The NO-NONSENSE GUIDE to

# SEXUAL DIVERSITY

'Publishers have created lists of short books that discuss the questions that your average [electoral] candidate will only ever touch if armed with a slogan and a soundbite. Together [such books] hint at a resurgence of the grand educational tradition... Closest to the hot headline issues are *The No-Nonsense Guides*. These target those topics that a large army of voters care about, but that politicos evade. Arguments, figures and documents combine to prove that good journalism is far too important to be left to (most) journalists.'

Boyd Tonkin,
*The Independent*,
London

**About the author**
**Vanessa Baird** is a co-editor of the New Internationalist magazine.

**Other titles in the series**
*The No-Nonsense Guide to Animal Rights*
*The No-Nonsense Guide to Climate Change*
*The No-Nonsense Guide to Conflict and Peace*
*The No-Nonsense Guide to Fair Trade*
*The No-Nonsense Guide to Globalization*
*The No-Nonsense Guide to Human Rights*
*The No-Nonsense Guide to International Development*
*The No-Nonsense Guide to Islam*
*The No-Nonsense Guide to Science*
*The No-Nonsense Guide to Tourism*
*The No-Nonsense Guide to World Health*
*The No-Nonsense Guide to World History*
*The No-Nonsense Guide to World Poverty*

**About the New Internationalist**
The **New Internationalist** is an independent not-for-profit publishing co-operative. Our mission is to report on issues of global justice. We publish informative current affairs and popular reference titles, complemented by world food, photography and gift books as well as calendars, diaries, maps and posters – all with a global justice world view.

If you like this *No-Nonsense Guide* you'll also love the **New Internationalist** magazine. Each month it takes a different subject such as *Trade Justice*, *Nuclear Power* or *Iraq*, exploring and explaining the issues in a concise way; the magazine is full of photos, charts and graphs as well as music, film and book reviews, country profiles, interviews and news.

To find out more about the **New Internationalist**, visit our website at
**www.newint.org**

# Foreword

SEXUAL DIVERSITY HAS been a familiar fact of life throughout recorded history. All societies have to find ways of living with it. Most fail dismally.

In the industrialized North for the past several centuries the main focus for regulating and controlling it has been through fashioning a sharp divide between heterosexual ('normal') and homosexual ('abnormal', 'perverted', 'deviant') patterns. This has been sanctified by churches and states, sustained by education, medicine, welfare services, popular prejudice – and even the patterns of housing.

In other parts of the world, diversity has been controlled in two broad ways. In some cultures, homosexual practices have been allowed as part of the rites of passage from adolescence to adulthood – though always under the dominance of traditional male privilege. In others, specialized roles have been created – especially in religious rites and prostitution – for the intersexual, effeminate or unconventional man.

But whatever the patterns across the world there are some common features of regulation and control. They are usually concerned with male sexuality. They generally subordinate sexual difference to traditional values. They have tended to marginalize, and usually condemn, those who do not conform to the culture's norms. Yet they have always failed to eradicate sexual diversity amongst women and men.

What is different today is that those who were regularly silenced by history have erupted into it. Across the world, the sexually marginalized have made claim to human rights, equality and justice. They have confronted prejudice, discrimination, homophobia and repression in different ways, depending on the local situation. In the rich countries, by and large, a new climate of relative toleration has developed since the 1960s, though by no means full acceptance. In many other parts of the world, gays, lesbians, and trans-gendered people are still regularly beaten or even murdered for their sexualities. The new visibility of sexually different people has in some parts of the world become a justification for heightened homo-phobic attacks. Individuals have to struggle to express their sexualities.

There are many local patterns, and many continu-ing injustices. But there is now also a global discourse of resistance, and of claims to justice, and elements of a globalized culture. The world is changing, and the speed of change is ever increasing.

Vanessa Baird's lively and compelling *No-Nonsense Guide to Sexual Diversity* provides a powerful over-view of this changing world. This second edition, with much new material, reflects the dramatic nature of the transformations taking place in an ever more globalized world, with new sites of conflict around sexuality and gender balanced by new opportunities for the recognition of the right to be able to express your sexuality in your own way.

The book is both a historical and cross-cultural account, and an intervention in contemporary debates. It reflects, and contributes to, the struggle to recognize and respect sexual diversity – to value it as a vital part of our common humanity.

*Jeffrey Weeks*
Professor of Sociology
London South Bank University
London, UK

# CONTENTS

# Introduction

THESE ARE DIZZYING, confusing times to be writing about sexual diversity.

We are witnessing change at an unprecedented pace.

Long gone, or so it sometimes seems, are the days when homosexuality and transgender were barely mentioned in anything other than hushed whispers, complex euphemisms and unfinished sentences.

The drive to extend rights and acceptance of gay and transgender people has had visible results in many countries. Sexual minority people are not just out and confident – they are winning basic civil rights and protections against discrimination in everyday areas such as employment, education, parenting and family life.

It is perhaps inevitable that this is provoking kicks and screams of violent outrage from some quarters. Never in the history of social change – be it the abolition of the slave trade or the emancipation of women – have there not been those vehemently opposed.

But in recent times rows about sexual diversity have become center stage in national and international debates to a quite extraordinary degree. Sexuality is being drawn into debates about the 'war on terror', about clashing or competing beliefs and value systems, about tradition, multiculturalism and globalization.

And while life has improved for many lesbian, gay, bisexual and transgender people in several countries, there has been an actual increase in the number of states where homosexuality is illegal and punishable by death.

Visibility is the oxygen of equality. But it can also be a hazard. And the targeting, and violent killing, of sexually diverse people who dare to organize and campaign for the right to be themselves, to love according to their desire and nature, is a growing trend in some parts of the world and in some communities.

What is it about this issue that stokes such controversy and such powerful feelings?

The intention of this revised and updated book is to shine a light on a fascinating but fraught area of human experience and the global responses to it. That involves looking into various 'hidden' histories – which may be quite a bit more 'queer' than most people realize – as well as the contemporary situation. It involves looking at religious as well as scientific views; and of course at the culture, psychology and politics, of both sexual diversity and of homophobia.

Often focusing on a minority culture ends up telling you as much about the majority culture in which it exists. The homosexual perspective calls into question heterosexual norms and assumptions; transgender individuals challenge a whole stack of assumptions about what gender is, why it matters and how it works in society.

Which is why a book dealing with lesbian, gay, bisexual, transgender or intersex people is not just about these minorities – it's about society in general. It's about all of us.

*Vanessa Baird*
Oxford, 2007

---

## Terms – a simple guide:
- sex has to do with your body, it's your biology: for example, female, male, intersex (hermaphrodite).
- gender is what you are in society: for example, woman, man, transgendered or trans person.
- sexuality is to do with desire and orientation: for example heterosexual, homosexual, bisexual.

**Other commonly used terms:**
- Transgender or Trans: includes transvestites (cross-dressers), transsexuals (whether they have had sex-reassignment therapy or not), intersexuals and eunuchs.
- LGBT: lesbian, gay, bisexual and transgender. This is the way many sexual minority organizations now describe themselves. Some now use LGBTI – to include intersexual as a distinctive category to describe people born with one of many medically recognized intersex conditions. ■

# 1 Global overview

**The world's coming out... globalization's sexual effects... the internet... identity, poverty and curious accommodations.**

AS WILLIAM HERNANDEZ chatted I could make out the shapes of armed men moving around on the other side of the large panes of frosted glass behind him. Earlier he had asked me why they were here. 'For our protection,' I'd replied. There had been violent threats from a fascist group.

He'd given a weary sort of smile. It was 'home from home' for William, who had just flown in from El Salvador for the Rome gathering of international sexual minority activists.

'Twenty of our comrades have been killed,' he said, describing the situation faced by him and other members of the San Salvador-based organization *Entre Amigos* (Between Friends). 'Only two deaths were investigated by the police.'

An attempt was made on his own life; he received further death threats. The office of *Entre Amigos* was broken into and the files ransacked. When he went to the police to ask for protection he was told that he should not expect them to protect people like him.

William got in touch with the human-rights organizations Amnesty International and the International Gay and Lesbian Human Rights Commission. They started an international campaign and *Entre Amigos* finally got police protection.

The story of *Entre Amigos* shows how far and how fast sexual diversity politics has moved. It indicates that a growing number of sexual minority people are not willing to keep quiet, even in the most hostile climates. And it demonstrates the effectiveness of international networking.

But it also shows that even battles that have

been fought and won may need to be fought time and again. For the incident above happened in the year 2000. By 2007, William was again appealing for international action as once more he had been threatened at gunpoint by a man warning him to stop his sexuality rights work 'or I'll kill you before you get married'. The offices of *Entre Amigos* were broken into and written threats – 'fags die' and 'this is what you deserve' – were left.[1]

*Entre Amigos* is an organization of our times. It symbolizes the social and political potential of sexual diversity and sex rights in today's world as well as the challenge of operating in a hostile environment.

'We have lesbians, bisexuals, transvestites, transsexuals... we have no intersexuals but I'm sure we will in time... The people who use our center are some of the city's most marginalized. They include prostitutes, drug addicts, thieves...' Diversity and social inclusiveness are, says William, central to the organization's ethos.

## Globalizing the issue

When I first started working on lesbian and gay issues in the late 1980s I was hard pushed to find people to write about the subject in Africa, Asia, and the Middle East. Homosexuality was all but invisible in many parts of the world.

I remember broaching the topic with a Kenyan aid worker who smiled knowingly as she told me that I would not find anyone to write about homosexuality in her country for the simple reason that it did not exist. 'It's not in our culture,' she explained.

Some still maintain this line – but they do so in the face of an explosion of evidence to the contrary.

At the 2007 meeting of the World Social Forum in Nairobi, African lesbian and gay speakers made sure that no-one got away with trying to pretend they did not exist, despite attempts to silence them.

## Global overview

'The love that dare not speak its name' is echoing around the world. In popular culture, lesbian and gay characters and themes have become commonplace – even in countries with traditions of repression. Some of the most popular singers in Turkey are gay. Cuba, which used to imprison or exile gay and lesbian people, now sees homosexuality depicted in contemporary literature and internationally acclaimed films such as *Strawberry and Chocolate*.

In the news media too, homosexuality is a hot topic. The Ugandan tabloid *Red Pepper* recently ran a campaign inviting readers to write in and expose lesbians and gay men in order to 'rid the country of this evil'. The paper's outing of 58 alleged lesbians and gay men put them at considerable risk and prompted protests internationally.[2]

Similarly, when Iran tortured and hanged teenagers Mahmoud Asgari and Ayaz Marhoni for being gay in 2005, shocking images of the scene were beamed around the world. In response Sweden and The Netherlands stopped extraditing lesbian and gay asylum-seekers to Iran.[3]

On the legal front several countries have followed the example set by South Africa and Ecuador and outlawed discrimination on the grounds of sexual orientation. In a similar vein, many have followed Denmark's lead and introduced civil partnership or marriage for same-sex couples.

The United Nations, which for decades maintained a stony silence on the issue of sexuality, has become a regular stage for fights over sex rights. When Brazil tried to get a ban on discrimination on the grounds of sexual orientation included in the UN charter in 2003 it was blocked by an alliance of Muslim states and the Vatican.

But in 2006 a new attempt was made by Norway which delivered a landmark statement on human rights, sexual orientation and gender identity on behalf of 54 states. The statement condemned human rights violations against people because of their sexual orientation or gender identity and called upon the UN to pay due attention to such violations. These violations include use of the death penalty, torture, criminal sanctions, police harassment, rape, beatings, denials of expression, raids and closures of NGOs, discrimination in education, employment, health and housing.

'Too often in the past these human rights abuses have passed in silence,' said Chris Sidoti, Director of the International Service for Human Rights. 'Now the era of invisibility is over.'[4]

## The internet
Most dramatic in its capacity to globalize information about sexual diversity has been a technological development: the internet.

Along with the satellite dish, the internet has enabled many who identity as lesbian, gay or transgender, to realize that they are not alone, and this has helped them to find models in other non-homophobic societies.

Providing they can access the internet, lesbian and gay Africans now have excellent websites, such as *Behind the Mask*, dealing with their issues on their continent; Asians have several including *Trikone*, while there are now a number of sites in Arabic catering for lesbian, gay and transgendered people living under Muslim laws. Some sites help lesbians and gay men to arrange 'marriages of convenience'.

'If it wasn't for the internet,' says Salim, a young Egyptian man, 'I wouldn't have come to accept my sexuality.'[5]

So effective has the internet been that the authorities in some countries have been trying to bar access to gay websites.

'The government blocks a lot of sites,' one gay Saudi Arabian told OutUK, 'but if you know how to navigate the Net, you can get around.'[5]

More sinister is the increasing use of the internet by the authorities to entrap sexual minority people. This is happening in Egypt, Iran, Palestine and Iraq. There have been cases where police and others have arranged to meet gay men via the net. On meeting, however, victims have been blackmailed, arrested, beaten or in some cases, murdered.

---

### The internet – lifesaver or snare?

Police in the city of Lucknow used the internet to entrap four men and jail them under India's colonial-era sodomy law in 2005. Undercover agents, posing as gay men on an internet website, entrapped one man, then forced him to call others.

According to Human Rights Watch the case illustrates an increasingly frequent phenomenon: fears around sexual diversity intersecting with fears relating to information diversity. ∎

IGLHRC/ Human Rights Watch

---

### 'Tradition' kicks in

All of this could be said to reflect a globalization of the struggle for human rights.

But globalization and human rights are not natural companions. The economic globalization process that has gone into overdrive since the end of the Cold War has generally undermined human rights by privileging the richest at the expense of the poorest. The effects on organized labor as multinational corporations swoop into countries with the lowest wages and most lax labor laws, only to swoop out again as soon as a contractor elsewhere offers a fatter profit margin, are well known. The flattening of difference, the Disney-fication of cultures and economies across the world is there for all to see.

The media has given gays and lesbians in Lima or Jakarta images of Western gay culture that they can relate to more easily than the heterosexual norms they are pressed to live by, but at a cost: chiefly that the world's media is in the hands of so very few Western corporations.

The strongest challenge to such globalization of culture – and the commodification of sex like never before – appears to have come from countries that have embraced religious fundamentalism.

As Dennis Altman points out in his book *Global Sex*, the rapid pace of change has produced a panic reaction which has taken the form of going back to (highly selective, often invented) 'indigenous' or 'traditional values'. He predicts that 'as the world becomes more and more subject to the influence and images of consumer capitalism, the attempts to reject globalization may well become more savage.[6]

The traditional values invoked are rarely those associated with caring, sharing and compassion. More often they reinforce authoritarianism, patriarchy, nationalism and xenophobia. Its victims are predominantly women, and racial and sexual minorities.

Homosexuality is illegal in more than 80 states in the world. It is punished by death in around 10 of these, where Muslim sharia law is applied. The situation for individuals who stray from the sexual rules and norms in these countries has got worse in the past decade as more punitive interpretations of sharia law are being applied.

For example, in the past sharia laws against same-sex or transgender activity were rarely invoked in Saudi Arabia because of the practical requirement that four witnesses were needed for a prosecution to go ahead.

Today the witness requirements have been relaxed and prosecutions are far more common. Some executions have taken place in the past 10 years but punishment mostly takes the form of imprisonment and flogging.

In Iran punishment has been far more severe with

---

**SEX and the LAW**

• In Iran, Saudi Arabia, Mauritania, Sudan and Yemen homosexuality is a capital offence. In parts of Nigeria, Somalia, Pakistan, Iraq and in Chechnya the application of sharia law means that homosexuality is punishable by death.

• In 111 countries homosexuality is legal; some of these have laws against discrimination. In around 85 it is illegal.

• In 9 countries the legal situation is unclear.

Note: See appendix for a country-by-country survey

---

an estimated 200 people a year executed because of their sexual orientation.[7]

Even in countries which are lustily embracing economic globalization and free-market ideology, there have been conservative reactions to the pace of social change. Malaysia and Indonesia have seen a trumpeting of traditional 'Asian values' as opposed to those of the West. The values lauded however are those that keep women in a servile position and reject local homosexual and transgendered populations. Malaysian premier Mohamad Mahathir's imprisonment of his chief political opponent Anwar Ibrahim on sodomy charges, exploited the idea that homosexuality is foreign corruption that insults Asian values and must be rejected.

In Zimbabwe, Mugabe's stance was anti-Western and anti-gay in one breath. Both Mugabe and Mahathir shored up weakening political power by adopting a strong anti-colonial stance, while ironically using old colonial anti-sodomy laws to 'purify' their nations.

The message is this: deviance from heterosexuality is a foreign thing, un-African or un-Asian or un-Arab; it has no place in these societies.

**We are everywhere?**
To which the usual answer – and a traditional rallying cry of the gay liberation movement – is that sexual minorities 'are everywhere'. The scores of groups that

have sprung up in the developing world during the past few years, which use words like 'gay' or 'lesbian' or 'transgender' in their names, certainly seem to reflect this notion. But it is not quite that simple.

The idea of a gay identity or transgender identity is not universal; and the suggestion that it is can be seen as a piece of Western ethno-centricity. Many people in the South do indeed identify as 'gay' in much the same way as do many in the rich world. Some in the South may be middle-class city-dwellers or belong to élites which have easy access to international ideas and media. Maybe they have visited North America, Europe, Australia and Aotearoa/New Zealand or even studied there.

Many have not. Take Vimlesh, a working class woman in India who dresses in male attire. She remarks: 'You ask me if I have heard the word "lesbian". No I have not heard it, till you explained it to me. I consider myself male, I am attracted to women.'[8]

Others prefer their own local terms to foreign sounding words like 'gay'. The word 'kothi' is used by Indians who either don't speak English or who want to emphasize that their sexuality is indigenous, not a 'Western import'.

But many more people in the South actually engage in same-sex sex without identifying themselves as any type of person, sexually speaking, at all. They *do* homosexuality, if you like, without *being* homosexuals.

This is true of many of the men-who-have-sex-with-men interviewed by writer Jeremy Seabrook in the Indian subcontinent. In the Delhi park where he conducted his research Seabrook was given a number of reasons why men sought men as sexual partners. They included: the absence of women among migrant communities, the availability of young male prostitutes and the belief that sex with men is 'safer' than vaginal sex which many were convinced posed the only danger of HIV or STD transmission. But the men did not say they had sex with men because they were gay or homosexual. By the same token, some cultural practices and perceptions Seabrook found were 'bewilderingly unfamiliar to the West'.[9]

There is, across the world, a great plethora of such practices. And there are many homoerotic cultures that thrive without any need of Western notions of 'gay identity'. For example, Afro-Surinamese women who call each other *mati* have long-term, intense, often open sexual relationships with each other in between or along with their sexual relationships with men. But a *mati* is not considered a distinctive kind of woman equivalent to a lesbian.[10]

In some cultures, style and gender identity is what counts. In Indonesia anthropologist Evelyn Blackwood found that only women who adopted an ultra-masculine style (closer to 'transgendered' than Western concepts of 'butch') were considered true *tombois* – lesbians. Their more feminine partners did not earn this title, and were often considered basically heterosexual, whatever their actual sexual practice.

Elsewhere it may come down to what sexual role you take – or are perceived to take. Among men in Latin America, a distinction is made (often falsely) between the macho role of the insertive partner and the feminized role of the receptive partner. The latter is viewed as a *marecon*, 'not a real man' and is stigmatized as such. The stigma does not attach in the same way to the active or insertive partner who is viewed socially as a 'real man'. 'A man fucks' is how it is formulated.

One young Guatemalan inserter expresses it thus: 'If I let him fuck me I'd probably like it and I'd do it again and then I'd be queer.'[11]

Ironic, though not surprising, is the common complaint of 'feminine' or transvestite male prostitutes that their macho 'real men' clients want to be the receptive partner.[9]

In many cultures same-sex sexualities are 'transgenderal' in that they put gender identity in question. In Latin America, for example, female terms such as *loca* or *bicha* are used for gay males.

In China, which has a growing sexual-minority scene, very few relate to the idea of a homosexual identity. Writer and academic Chou Wah-shan reports that the most popular contemporary word for lesbian, bisexual and gay people is *tongzhi* meaning 'comrade'. In the course of conducting 200 interviews with a wide range of *tongzhi* people, not one of his informants described themself as a *tongxinglina* – a homosexual.[12]

According to Chou, the reluctance to take up a homosexual identity should not necessarily be seen as a product of homophobia. Many Chinese *tongzhi* stress that sexuality is only one integral part of life and does not mark them as categorically different people. Traditional Chinese culture has a more fluid conception of sexuality and treats homosexuality as an option that most people can experience, rather than as something restricted to a sexual minority having fixed, inherent traits. As Hong Kong-based activist Nelson Ng puts it: 'Sometimes I like noodles, sometimes I like rice – and sometimes, if I am very hungry, I like both!'

But gay identities and communities similar to those in the West are taking shape in new parts of the world. In the North African cities of Rabat, Casablanca and Tunis gay men are living out their sexuality and trying out long term relationships – a novelty according to researcher Vincenzo Patane.[11]

An increasing number of lesbians in India are doing the unthinkable and escaping the traditions of family and compulsory marriage to set up home together, usually in big cities.

For them sexuality is not just something they do – it is something they are.

## Rich world, poor world, queer world

As always, the freedom to live your life as you choose is heavily determined by social and economic factors. This is true for sexual minority people living in poverty, be it in the North or in the South. It can be much harder to be openly lesbian or gay or transgender if you are poor. Privacy is a luxury and living out a non-conforming sexuality is rarely an option if you have to share your sleeping quarters with several family members.

In most societies 'the family' is the strongest opponent to homosexuality, which is seen as a threat to it. But in poorer countries and communities, people are entirely dependent on family networks for survival. Family, marriage and children are, in the words of Jeremy Seabrook, 'the very tissue of survival. You don't have to go very far on the streets of Sao Paulo, Dhaka and Nairobi to see the effects upon those excluded from that security'.

Lack of a welfare or social security 'safety net' also makes being 'out' at work very risky. Not only do few countries have any protection from discrimination on the grounds of sexual orientation, but those who lose their jobs because they have been 'discovered' are once again thrown back onto their families, who may reject them too because of their sexuality.

Not surprisingly many sexual minority people in poor countries end up homeless and reliant on prostitution for survival. Most survive in urban settings, where family bonds are weaker. The process of urbanization, viewed so negatively by many development commentators, has been liberating for oppressed groups such as sexual minorities, and to a large extent women too.

The lives and cultures that these working class men

and women forge for themselves on the margins of society often go unrecorded and unnoticed.

With the exception of HIV/AIDS organizations, these lesbian and gay urban poor are ignored by voluntary and government agencies.

Even local women's groups and some LGBT groups fail to reach them. When middle-class researcher Maya Sharma tells an Indian lesbian about the leafleting her organization did in response to the homophobic furore surrounding Deepa Mehta's lesbian-themed film *Fire* the woman responds by saying:

'I never saw such pamphlets. You should distribute them in the slums.'

Lesbian, gay and transgender individuals exist in communities all over the world, whether rich or poor. If they can 'come out' they may to some extent change the attitudes of those around them – even in the most unpromising environments.

William Hernandez, whose story opened this chapter, comes from a working-class background, in a country with an intensely homophobic social climate. But his family came round to accepting him and his sexuality – 'even the most "square" ones did' – and are now, he says, very supportive. Simple, humane accommodations do take place. Chou Wahshan reports the case of a young man whose lover lives in the family home with his parents who, without the word 'homosexuality' being mentioned, have just accepted the partner as a son-in-law because they can see how good the relationship is for their previously suicidal son.[12]

## Solidarity

To categorize the global situation as: 'rich world equals tolerance, equals visible sexual minorities, equals gay identity' and the 'poor world' as the opposite of this immediately invites exceptions. Saudi Arabia, one of the richest countries in the world, has some of the most extreme punishments against homosexuality. Niger, one of the poorest, recognizes same-sex marriages.

In fact some of the most repressive laws came from the rich world in the first place – the British Empire was particularly generous in this respect. Evangelizing Christianity played a major role in demonizing the sexual deviant and trying to obliterate same-sex traditions that existed in indigenous American, Asian or African cultures.

Recent times have seen international sexual-minority solidarity flourish. Since 1991 Amnesty International has included persecution on the grounds of sexual orientation within its mandate. Persecution on grounds of sexuality has been accepted as a reason for granting asylum in a number of countries, though practice rarely follows the principle.

The International Lesbian and Gay Association (ILGA) has 350 or more member groups across five continents. Like Amnesty, the International Gay and Lesbian Human Rights Commission (ILGHRC) has contributed to the perception of sexual minority rights as human rights and mobilized specific international solidarity campaigns. Smaller organizations, such as OutRage! have carried out effective, often headline grabbing campaigns – such as Peter Tatchell's attempted citizen's arrest of President Robert Mugabe – aimed at supporting LGBTI people living in the most difficult circumstances. Solidarity is increasingly taking the form of urging governments not to deport sexual minority asylum seekers back to countries where they will be persecuted.

The fact that international activists are keeping an eye on human rights abuses against LGBTI citizens and publicizing cases where they can, does not go unheeded in countries where oppression is greatest. A gay activist in Iran writes: 'We express our appreciation and admiration for the united efforts world-wide... in support of Iranian LGBT people, against homophobic oppression and all executions in Iran. These efforts give us Iranian LGBTs hope and inspiration. It is good for our morale. Please do not stop.'[4]

In the words of pioneering Indian gay activist Ashok Row Kavi: 'We are truly international and we are a truly planetary minority.'

Today, we can talk of a global sexual minority movement – while recognizing a total lack of uniformity and a dazzling wealth of diversity.

1 Amnesty International, 2007. 2 www.blacklooks.org 3 http://www.365gay.com/newscon05/07/073105holland.htm 4 www.ilga.org/news 5 *Unspeakable Love – Gay and Lesbian Life in the Middle East*, Brian Whitaker, Saqi, 2006 6 *Global Sex*, Dennis Altman, The University of Chicago Press, 2001. 7 Homan www.homanla.org 8 *Loving Women – Being Lesbian in Unprivileged India*, Maya Sharma Yoda Press, 2006 9 It's what you do', Jeremy Seabrook, *New Internationalist*, October 2000. 10 *Female Desires*, Evelyn Blackwood and Saskia E Wieringa eds, Columbia University Press, 1999. 11 *Gay Life and Culture – a World History*, Robert Aldrich ed., Thames and Hudson, 2006. 12 *Different Rainbows*, Peter Drucker ed, Gay Men's Press, 2000. 13 *Crimes of Hate, Conspiracies of Silence*, Amnesty International, 2001.

# 2 'The Revolution's here!'

**The birth of the movement... early pioneers... 'sexual inversion'... gay lib... lesbian separatism... S & M sex radicals... South Africa's pride... AIDS action... queer politics... wedding bells... Palestinian pioneers... toward LGBTI diversity.**

28 JULY 1969. It's a hot, muggy summer's night in New York. The Stonewall Inn bar in Greenwich Village is heaving with gay men, lesbians and drag queens in all their finery.

Suddenly, at about 1 am, the lights come on. People stop dancing; it's a police raid. The Morals Squad is back. Customers are led out and 'cattled' up against the police vans. They are pushed up against grates and fences.

But tonight something is different. Instead of going obediently into the waiting paddy vans some people start throwing pennies, nickels and quarters. Then some bottles start to fly. There's a fracas as the crowd resists the police and shouts 'gay power' and other slogans. The police take refuge and barricade themselves into the building; they call for reinforcements. Protesters rip up a parking meter and begin to ram the door.

Sylvia Rivera was there and remembers it well: 'We were not taking any more of this shit. We had done so much for other movements. It was time... I remember when someone threw a Molotov cocktail I thought: "My God, the revolution is here. The revolution is finally here." I always believed we would fight back, I just knew we would fight back. I just didn't know it would be that night.'

The protests continued for several nights running, and were followed by further protests and marches. Something had begun.[1,2]

These 'Stonewall Riots' are often seen as the ignition

point – the Boston Tea Party of the Gay Liberation movement in the West. Indeed they were charged with an almost sacred meaning. But this was not really the first event of its kind. Paris and Amsterdam had seen similar outbursts in the previous year.

It was, perhaps, to be expected. The 1960s had been a decade of radicalism. The influence of the Black Civil Rights and Women's movements was tremendous. As feminists examined and challenged sexism, and black activists fought racism under slogans such as 'Black is Beautiful', it was indeed time to challenge the prejudice against homosexuals.

## Early pioneers and the birth of 'homosexuality'

But even these 20th century acts of rebellion by gays and lesbians had a precursor a century earlier of, arguably, greater significance. Karl Heinrich Ulrichs, a German law student, journalist and secretary to various civil servants and diplomats, had single-handedly urged for the repeal of all laws that criminalized same-sex sexual activity.[3]

In May 1862 his acquaintance Johann Baptist von Schweitzer was arrested for public indecency. Ulrichs wrote a defense and sent it to him, but it was confiscated by the authorities. Ulrichs, who had been attracted to men since his early teens, decided that now was the time to solve the 'riddle' of his sexuality.

In 1864 he published his *Researches on the Riddle of 'Man-Manly' Love*. He used a pseudonym in deference to his relatives, but acknowledged his identity in 1868. By 1879 he had published 12 volumes on this subject. His 'scientific' inspiration was contemporary embryology, which discovered that the sex organs are undifferentiated in the earliest stages of the development of the fetus. By analogy homosexual desire was just as 'natural' as this containment of the opposite sex within the developing embryo. He argued that same-sex desire was congenital and therefore it was inhumane for the law to punish homosexuals as if these were crimes willfully chosen.

Ulrichs was politically motivated by fear that the Prussians would invade Hanover and impose the anti-homosexual statute of the Prussian Penal Code – which is exactly what went on to happen. He was briefly imprisoned for expressing outspoken Social Democrat views and in 1867 the police confiscated his collection of homosexual research material.

He was ridiculed in the press, and forced to leave Hanover on his release from prison. He moved to Bavaria and in August 1867 at the Congress of German Jurists in Munich gave a speech for homosexual rights which marked the beginning of the public homosexual emancipation movement in Germany. But in 1872 Prussian anti-homosexual legislation extended to all of unified Germany. In 1880 Ulrichs felt compelled to leave the country, and he settled in Italy for the remaining 15 years of his life.

Ulrichs was not however responsible for the word 'homosexuality'. That was the invention of German-Hungarian Karoly Maria Kertbeny (born Benkert in 1824). It is the compound of the Greek word homo (same) and the medieval Latin sexualis (sexual). Although Kertbeny claimed to be heterosexual, his long-term anonymous and pseudonymous campaign for gay rights suggests otherwise.

It took several more decades for the word 'homosexual' to make its way into the English language. It did not appear until 1891, in John Addington Symonds' *A Problem in Modern Ethics* where he used the phrase 'homosexual instincts'. His book was privately printed in an edition of 10 copies. In *Sexual Inversion* (1897) British sexologist Havelock Ellis together with Symonds (whose name was removed from the title page after the first edition) popularized the idea of 'inversion' as an inborn pathological gender anomaly.

In the early years of the 20th century, the British socialist and gay pioneer Edward Carpenter (1844-1929) published his polemical book *The Intermediate Sex*. It was to have a profound impact upon women as well as men. The second-generation feminist Frances Wilder in 1912 was advocating self-restraint and abstinence in the radical *Freewoman* magazine but only three years later Carpenter's book helped her to realize that she was not simply a feminist, but a lesbian feminist. She wrote to him: 'I have recently read with much interest your book entitled *The Intermediate Sex* and it has lately dawned on me that I myself belong to that class and I write to ask if there is any way of getting in touch with others of the same temperament.'³

## Wilde's 'madness'

Oscar Wilde's high-profile contribution came during his 1895 trial in which he famously defended 'the love that dare not speak its name' comparing it to the love of David for Jonathan. He spoke of its beauty and nobility with reference to works by Plato, Michelangelo and Shakespeare. 'It was a theatrical tour de force,' comments Rictor Norton wryly, 'but it did not stand up to the testimony of boy prostitutes.'

As a homosexual man Wilde saw himself as part of a cultural élite opposed to modern philistine heterosexuality. He was later to issue a retraction and call his condition 'a madness' but that did not save him from jail and two years' hard labor. Although he is held up today as a 'gay martyr', Wilde did not in practice further the cause for decriminalizing homosexuality in his own times. If anything attitudes became even more hostile.

Radclyffe Hall's pioneering lesbian novel *The Well of Loneliness* was also the subject of scandal and a court case when it was published in 1928. The book was a plea for tolerance for 'inverts' who led difficult lives of pain and sacrifice – it did not actually show happy homosexual love which Hall herself was to enjoy for 30 years with her partner Una Trowbridge. But it brought to light a deeply hidden subject, to the extent that one of the reasons the Lord Chancellor, Lord Birkenhead, gave for banning it was that 'of every 1,000 women 999... have never even heard a whisper of these practices'.[4]

Meanwhile, in Germany, the gay sexologist Magnus Hirschfeld had set up the Institute for Sexual Science in Berlin. It was to become a source of inspiration and information for gay people internationally. His library contained 12,000 books, 35,000 photos and countless manuscripts – all destroyed by Nazi students on 6 May 1933.[3]

The clamp-down on homosexuals both during and after the 1939-45 war provoked another wave of political activism. In the US the Daughters of Bilitis and Mattachine Society organized lesbians and gay men for mutual support. With the rise of more militant factions, the movement for gay liberation had a surge of energy in the 1960s. The abandonment of the word 'homosexual' – with its medical connotations – and the adoption of the word 'gay' as a self description marked a crucial stage in the development of a politicized sexual identity.

The tip-toeing of the homophile movements was replaced by the bolder chant: 'Gay is good'. Gay people came 'out of the closets'. Gay liberation was not to be won by élites speaking softly in corridors of power, but by ordinary people taking to the street and demanding decriminalization and freedom. Public marches forced the issue onto heterosexual public consciousness not only in North America, Australia, Aotearoa/New Zealand and Europe but also in some countries of the South, such as Mexico and Argentina. Politically radical 'gay liberation fronts' were formed in various countries, preaching peace, love and revolution.

## Taking the labrys* to patriarchy

Third-wave feminists were also making their mark. With their bold and trenchant analyses of patriarchy, radical feminists offered new insights. The feminist slogan 'the personal is political' was an eye-opener for many and made legitimate raising issues of inequality that were previously easy to dismiss as 'personal' or 'private'.

Feminism encouraged both women and men to depart from gender stereotypes. It provided new models in terms of consciousness-raising and non-hierarchical forms of organizing. These were to become features of radical AIDS activism, the anti-nuclear movement, and the ecology movement as well as the lesbian and gay liberation movements.

Lesbians made radical contributions to the women's movement during the 1970s and 1980s. Activists and writers such as Audre Lorde, Adrienne Rich and Mary Daly produced a brand of feminism that was to shake the liberal heterosexual establishment and provoke a deeper questioning about strategies for resisting patriarchy. Adrienne Rich rattled cages – and opened eyes – with her publication of *Compulsory Heterosexuality and Lesbian Existence* which was to become something of a manifesto for 'political lesbianism'.[5] For many feminists, lesbianism became a logical next step in their struggle to liberate themselves from male domination. This became crystalized in the slogan 'feminism is the theory, lesbianism is the practice'.

Rich talked of a 'lesbian continuum' which included all women who considered themselves 'women-centered' and believed that being in a sexual relation with a man would always keep them entrapped or compromised. Not all these women would necessarily be sexually attracted to other women, but they could

---

* *ancient Cretan double-headed ax, a popular lesbian symbol.*

still consider themselves political lesbians.

Sex radicals like Pat Califia and Joan Nestle derided this rather asexual approach to lesbianism. They wanted sex to be brought back center-stage. Califia and others effectively did so by promoting lesbian sado-masochism as opposed to the 'vanilla' sex of mainstream and political lesbianism. Heated debates ensued, but the sex radicals can be said to have had a lasting, sex-positive effect on contemporary lesbian culture.[6]

Meanwhile the position of women within the 'gay liberation' movement was often fraught. Men, including gay men, were part of the dominant culture that oppressed women and sexism existed within the movement as much as anywhere. During the 1970s lesbians around the world formed their own groups.

Many felt more at home within the women's movement – but a different set of prejudices was encountered there. Betty Friedan, US feminist and founder of the National Organization of Women (NOW), famously dismissed lesbianism as the 'lavender herring' of the women's movement. Others argued that discussing lesbianism would bring the women's movement into disrepute. Such attitudes, though less common, have not disappeared. Activist Norma Mogrovejo sees in the Mexican women's movement a 'profound internalized lesbophobia' and an assumption that heterosexist demands 'automatically include' lesbian concerns.[7]

At the 1995 UN Women's Conference attempts to get recognition for a woman's right to make her own decisions about her sexuality failed yet again. A renewed attempt at the 2000 Platform for Action suffered a similar fate, thanks to a coalition of US and African women opposing it on religious and cultural grounds.

However, in other fora women's movements have woken up to lesbianism as a political option. The

## Taboo-breaking Palestinian lesbian

'When I came out in 2003, I thought I would be killed or displaced from the community,' says Rauda Morcos, a poet and Palestinian Arab lesbian living in Israel. She received anonymous phonecalls, her car was damaged, and she lost her job working with young people. But she survived and went on to co-found Aswat, the first lesbian Palestinian organization of which she is now general co-ordinator.

'We wanted to find a way to break the silence that so many Palestinian lesbians face,' says Rauda. 'For this reason, it was important to bring women together in a safe place where they could talk about their own issues.'

The group operates within Israel but members also come across from the West Bank and Gaza for meetings which are held in different cities. Attending meetings is not easy: in Palestinian society lesbians and gay men are often viewed as traitors and extreme homophobic violence is common; in Israel, Palestinians are viewed as a security risk. Rauda is an outspoken critic of the Occupation. 'We're against any type of occupation,' she says. 'I don't want to be occupied as a Palestinian or as a woman or as a lesbian.'

A landmark moment for Palestinian lesbians came in March 2007 when Aswat held its first public conference in Haifa. Despite anti-lesbian protests, it was attended by 350 people and coincided with the publication of a new book in Arabic about lesbian and gay identity.

Most Aswat members, however still keep their lesbian identities secret in a society that, according to the group's website, 'has no mercy for sexual diversity'. ■

'Lesbian Palestinians Break Social Taboos', by Brenda Gazzar, WeNEWS, 3 April 2007 www.womensnews.org and 'A language no-one else is speaking' Glenn Kauth, Xtra!, 16 September 2004.

National Conference of the Women's Movement in India has had it as a regular topic of discussion since 1994. The publicity and protests surrounding the 1999 lesbian film *Fire* have done much to increase lesbian visibility and activism in India, with groups springing up around the country.

### Race and sexuality
Just as women's lib and gay lib have had various links and overlaps, so too have the struggles for racial and homosexual equality. Writers and activists like bell

hooks, Audre Lorde and James Baldwin explicitly linked the two (or more) struggles in their writings and in their lives.

The Civil Rights Movement in North America may have been an inspiration for other liberation movements, but that didn't stop gays and lesbians of color encountering racist attitudes within white-dominated gay organizations. Many felt that a false universalism was being promoted that did not reflect their reality. In the struggle to get their voices heard many formed separate groups. In the 1970s lesbians of color in the US formed political groups such as the National Black Feminist Organization and the first Black Lesbian Conference was held in San Francisco in 1980.

The linking of sexuality and race politics was most obvious in the war against apartheid. Back in 1986, current South African President Thabo Mbeki was saying: 'the ANC is indeed very firmly committed to removing all forms of discrimination and oppression in a liberated South Africa. The commitment must surely extend to the protection of gay rights.'[8]

Nelson Mandela made a point of mentioning the right to gay equality in his inaugural address after his election as president in 1994. This was later included in the Constitution – South Africa being the first country in the world to give its citizens the constitutional right not to be discriminated against on the grounds of sexual orientation.

Writer Mark Gevisser identifies three reasons why gay equality passed so smoothly into the Constitution. First the ANC leaders had a utopian progressive ideology and many of them would have come into contact with sexual liberation movements in the countries in which they were exiled. Second, South Africa's Anglican church is not generally homophobic. Its former Archbishop Desmond Tutu has been a prominent spokesperson for the rights of lesbians and gays. He even said: 'If the Church, after the victory over apartheid, is looking for a worthy moral crusade, then this is it; the fight against homophobia and heterosexism.' Third is the role of gay anti-apartheid activists. Foremost among these was Simon Nkoli. In the infamous Delmas treason trial of the mid-1980s, Nkoli disclosed his homosexuality, and eventually managed to gain the support of all his co-accused, several of whom are now senior members of the ANC Government.

Upon his release from prison in 1989, Nkoli founded GLOW, radically different from the gay organizations that preceded it in that it was a black organization. His major contribution was thus to counter the notion, prevalent in Africa, that homosexuality was not just un-Christian, but 'un-African', a white contamination of black society.[6]

As Patrick Lekota, ANC national chair and South African Defense Minister, said at the time of Nkoli's death from AIDS-related illness in 1999: 'How could we say that men and women like Simon who had put their shoulders to the wheel to end apartheid, how could we say that they should now be discriminated against?'

In Brazil too links have been made with others fighting for equality. The lesbian and gay organization SOMOS turned to the newly-constituted feminist and

---

### South African Drag Queen...

**on having an 'anti-discrimination on the grounds of sexual orientation' clause included in the country's Constitution:**

'My darling, it means sweet motherfucking nothing at all. You can rape me, rob me, what am I going to do if you attack me? Wave the Constitution in your face? I'm just a nobody black queen... But you know what? Ever since I heard about that Constitution, I feel free inside.' ■

Quoted by Mark Gevisser in *Different Rainbows*, Peter Drucker ed, Gay Men's Press, 2000.

black movements in the late 1970s to offer support. SOMOS members joined marches and protests against racial discrimination and in celebration of National Day and Black Consciousness distributed a leaflet that stated: 'The combativeness of Zumbi [an Afro-Brazilian who fought against slavery in the 17th century] is an example for all oppressed sectors of society in the fight for freedom. Coming from our own discrimination as homosexuals, we show our solidarity with all blacks in the struggle against racism.'

In Ecuador, the second country to include anti-discrimination on the grounds of sexual orientation in its Constitution, sexual minority groups have joined forces with the indigenous rights movement and campaigned on a broader human-rights platform.

## Inclusively Queer

In its early days the movement, in the West at least, used to be called 'gay'. Then it became 'lesbian and gay'. Then 'lesbian, gay and bisexual'. Now most organizations are referred to as LGBT – 'lesbian, gay, bisexual and transgender'. Some have now extended this to LGBTI to include 'intersexual' (see chapter 8).

Contributing, in its own particular way, to greater inclusiveness was Queer Politics. Emerging in the late 1980s and flourishing during the 1990s, it was a reaction to narrow identity politics, rigid categories and separate groups that had come to characterize the movement. With Queer Politics all identities – lesbian, gay, bisexual, transsexual, even some heterosexual – could merge into a general 'queerness'.

Queer Politics was a challenge to mainstream, 'straight' thinking of all kinds. But it was also opposed to the lesbian and gay movement's civil-rights approach. Whereas gay civil-rights strategists would utter the slogan 'We are everywhere' and believed that stressing the unthreatening 'normality' of lesbian and gay people as central to getting political room, the Queer approach was critical and oppositional. Its slogan: 'We're here, we're queer – get used to it!'

'Queer asserts in-your-face difference,' writes sociologist Joshua Gamson. 'Queer does not so much rebel against outsider status, it revels in it.'[6] Queer activism tends to take the form of street propaganda, acts of cultural non-conformity, and events such as multi-sexual, multi-genderal 'kiss-ins'. Its main activist organization is Queer Nation – a somewhat anarchic, decentralized affair which started in the US, spread to Britain and Australia, and has spawned various groups engaged in 'queeruption' anti-capitalist or anti-globalization activities.

Queer Theory had a stronger presence in academic institutions where it operated through rather abstract language. It derives its thinking partly from postmodernism and contemporary feminist philosophy, but mostly from the historical and social constructionist ideas of Michel Foucault – ideas that were also influential during the 1960s and 1970s era of gay lib.

Foucault saw homosexuality as a 'strategically situated marginal position' from where it might be possible to glimpse and devise new ways of relating to oneself and others. Queer Politics rejects gender oppression, but values its marginal, outsider perspective.

The ultimate challenge of queerness, however, is the questioning of the unity, stability and political utility of sexual and gender identities – even as they are used and assumed. In this, Queer Politics has more easily connected with and contributed to the development of a politics and theory of transgender. For transgendered and bisexual people queerness may serve as a useful umbrella term.

## Marriage – equality or sell-out?

There continues to be a fundamental tension between the belief in sexual diversity as something with a revolutionary and disruptive potential, and the quest for normality expressed in the notion that LGBT people 'are just like anyone else' and that all they are asking for is to be allowed to join the mainstream.

Nowhere is this more visible than in attitudes towards same-sex marriage.

'All my life I've been fighting for the right to be boring,' says Massachusetts Representative Barney Frank.[9]

He shares with many the view that civil partnerships, and better still marriage, are a mark of equality achieved, of a longed for normalcy.

But others see it as a sell-out to heterosexual values – another sign that gay people are, in the words of Larry Kramer, 'losing themselves in a massive vanilla heterosexual culture.'[9]

Kramer and others lament a squandering of political potential to upset the applecart, to radically challenge ideas about gender, sexuality, society.

Perhaps this is a role that is now being played to a

---

### Pink bells

First was Denmark in 1989 - soon to be followed by its Scandinavian neighbours. Today most of Europe – including the Czech Republic and Slovenia – recognizes same-sex partnerships for a range of purposes. Some, like Spain have gone the whole hog and approved same-sex marriage.

Latin America is following suit. Argentineans Cesar Gigliutti and Marcelo Suntheim became the first on the continent to have a civil union in 2003. Uruguay and Brazil extended partnership laws, while Mexico saw its first gay civil partnership in 2007.

Canada has full marriage and in Britain the popularity of a new domestic partnership law surpassed all expectations with 6,500 couples registering in the first year.

Meanwhile, in India, campaigners are arguing – with support from some religious leaders – that same-sex marriage is permissible under Hinduism as marriage is defined as a 'union of souls' and souls are not gendered. ■

Worldwide Trend of Recognizing Same-Sex Marriage, IGLHRC, 4 December 2006.

greater extent by transgender activists who question some of the most basic assumptions about what is male, what is female.

## Transgender agendas

In the past decade or so human-rights activists have become increasingly aware of the fact that transgendered people – especially sex workers – are particularly at risk from violence at the hands of police and other hostile groups. Various transgender organizations have emerged and many are now represented in the broader LGBT organizations. But the inclusion is by no means total and has not come easily. For many years the lesbian and gay movement saw transgender as a separate issue. Some argued that transsexualism was a product of stereotypical ways of thinking. If men could be more feminine and women more masculine, perhaps it would not be necessary to alter one's gender. Others felt transgendered people were being misled and exploited by the medical profession.

More hostile reactions came from some feminists – both lesbian and straight – who felt that male-to-female transsexuals, having been brought up male, could never know what it was like to be an oppressed female. In her book *The Transsexual Empire*, US academic Janice Raymond argued that transsexuals were the insidious tools of the patriarchal system, infiltrating women's circles and dividing women against themselves. 'All transsexuals rape women's bodies by reducing the real female form to an artifact, appropriating their bodies for themselves,' she wrote.

However the more inclusive politics of the 1990s led to new alliances and coalitions, some of which have been helpful to trans people. In Argentina, Brazil and Colombia, for example, the raising of trans issues by LGBT groups has led to changes in law and far greater public awareness of human-rights violations.

### 'The Revolution's here!'

Meanwhile influential sections of the women's movement have also changed position. In 1997, after being lobbied by the organization GenderPac and members of National Lesbian Rights, the US National Organization of Women (NOW) overwhelmingly passed a trans-inclusive resolution. One participant at the conference remarked that 'the transgender community is today's cutting edge... of exposing artificial gender constructs and breaking down stereotypes and barriers that divide us'.[10]

Indeed the contemporary feminist philosophy of women like Helene Cixous, Julia Kristeva, Luce Irigaray and Judith Butler has contributed much to a radical rethinking of the meaning of gender and transgender.

### Bisexual identities and strategies

Bisexuality has in recent times become more readily accepted within the lesbian and gay movement. The studies of Alfred Kinsey in the 1950s and Shere Hite in the 1970s and 1980s have shown that sexual desire for both sexes was so common that one could almost say that bisexuality is the norm – not a minority persuasion at all.

---

### They saw lipstick on the shower top

I am a 26-year old male and I have been a transvestite for over seven years. I have been outspoken about same–sex rights.

On December 1, 2005, I did an interview for World AIDS Day. My family watched the event and saw that I was gay. A friend called me and told me not to come home because they were planning something terrible for me. I did not return home for some time after this.

On another occasion, I wanted to go out for a party and I thought it would be better if I dressed up at home so that I would not be seen changing. My stepfather and brothers saw lipstick on the shower top. I was tied down and beaten all night long. Another time my stepfather poured hot cooking oil on my foot as punishment for being gay.' ■

Mohammed, Nigeria, IGLHRC, November 2006.

---

Comparatively few people openly identify as bisexual, though the number of teenagers who are doing so is increasing in places where there is greater acceptance of sexual diversity.

A large number of bisexuals actually live heterosexual lives while having gay sex – or desires – on the side. But among those who do openly identify are many who have demanded that they be explicitly recognized as a separate category and included as such within the lesbian and gay movement.

In one sense, the issue of bisexuality is the same as that of homosexuality – it's the homosexuality of the bisexual person that is discriminated against in society, not their heterosexuality. But within lesbian or gay groups bisexuals have experienced prejudice against them for their heterosexuality too.

Bisexuality is a different kind of issue in traditional societies where homosexuality is heavily punished and marriage virtually compulsory. There is a largely unspoken cultural acceptance of bisexuality in, for example, male migrant workers from Mozambique who may have a wife back home and a boyfriend in South Africa or men in Peru who, as photographer Annie Bungaroth reports, may decorously court a female fiancee, see her home at the end of the evening, and then go out with a male prostitute.

All sorts of accommodations occur. Writer Jeremy Seabrook recounts the case of a man in India who, when he returns to his home village near Varanasi, regularly has sex with his sister's husband. Married women too may be having covert lesbian relationships far more commonly than anyone imagines.

For many lesbians in more traditional societies, bisexuality is the only way to any degree of sexual and emotional authenticity. In countries such as India it is almost impossible for women to live independently of a family structure.

Many of the women who contact lesbian helplines

are married and desperate. Some are suicidal, reports the Delhi helpline Sangini. Accounts of women being killed by their husband on discovery of their lesbian relationship are not uncommon.

Meanwhile Indian feminists are viewing lesbianism and bisexuality with increasing interest. Flavia Agnes, an activist with the Forum Against Oppression of Women in Bombay, remarks: 'Many turn to lesbianism or bisexuality as a conscious political choice, for they cannot reconcile their radical understanding of themselves and other women in general with the inequality, exploitation, lack of respect and often blatant physical force that characterize typical heterosexual relationships whether in marriage or out of it.'[8]

## The response to AIDS

Profound in its effect on sexual minorities on all continents has been the AIDS epidemic. It has claimed the lives of so many, including gay activists, and weakened the movement as a result.

The scale of the current epidemic in Africa, where infection rates are one in four in some countries, does not invite positive comments on how the epidemic has been dealt with. But it would be wrong to overlook the good work that has been done and the speed with which some communities have been able to respond to the crisis.

When HIV/AIDS emerged in the early 1980s, lesbians and gays experienced a backlash of public opinion which labeled the syndrome the 'gay plague'. The struggle to get healthcare for a marginalized and now especially stigmatized group, led to an upsurge in community-based activism among lesbian and gay people. The fact that there already existed politically-aware gay and lesbian communities was a blessing. These provided the basis for new public health groups specifically to combat AIDS and promote the safer-sex message.

In Peru, Mexico and Nicaragua the gay movement was central to the emergence of AIDS support and education groups. In Brazil some gay groups joined with social workers, researchers, liberal clergy and people with AIDS to establish HIV/AIDS organizations. Where an organized gay base was lacking – as in much of Africa and the Indian subcontinent – it was much harder.

In some countries the gay presence in AIDS organizations had to be played down. For example, Action for AIDS in Singapore is described as 'de facto' a gay organization, but because very few people in it are prepared to come out as gay they must disguise this to some extent.[6]

It was not uncommon for gay-run AIDS organizations to receive government funding even in countries where homosexuality was outlawed. To some extent gay communities achieved 'legitimation through disaster', says Dennis Altman, who has studied community responses to the AIDS epidemic. But AIDS activists have also been ill-treated in countries where homosexuality is illegal: in Jamaica a nurse was killed for handing out condoms and in 2005 prominent AIDS activist Lenford 'Steve' Harvey was also murdered.

The links between vulnerability to AIDS and poverty, inequality and deprivation are now firmly established. AIDS flourished in an era of poverty caused by the debt crisis and structural adjustment programs that hit the poorest hardest. The sex trade, another product of poverty, also increased. Access to drugs for treating AIDS is also dependent on wealth. Little wonder then that the most marginalized people in the poorest places are most likely to become HIV-positive and die of AIDS.

However, in Brazil patents-busting initiatives have broken the domination of pharmaceutical giants

## 'The Revolution's here!'

Merck and Hoffman-la-Roche and made available cheaper generic drugs. Campaigners in Thailand have also taken on 'big pharma' and won. In 2002 a Thai court stripped the US drug company Bristol Myers Squibb of its exclusive right to manufacture the AIDS drug Videx in Thailand.[11]

Pharmaceutical companies that charge too much for their drugs and warmongers in Central Africa, where rape is being used as weapon, must bear much of the blame for the spread of infection there.

But governments are to blame too. Gay South African activist Zachie Achmat, who is HIV-positive, acquired hero status when he refused to take anti-retroviral drugs until they were made available to everyone in his country. After several years, Thabo Mbeki's government finally began to abandon its disastrous AIDS policy which had been based on an eccentric belief that there is no link between HIV and AIDS.[11]

The fact that the AIDS epidemic emerged in a world where gay and feminist politics were established meant that in some parts of both the poor and the rich world existing organizations and communities were able to respond and disseminate the safer sex message as rapidly as possible.

It may not seem like much in the face of suffering on the scale of Africa's, but it has limited damage elsewhere. And, as Dennis Altman points out: 'Such organizations could not have existed without the previous decade of organizing gay men and lesbians that followed the student riots in France in 1968 and the Stonewall Riots in 1969.'[6]

### Gone shopping?
A motley lot we are, marching down London's Oxford Street. Someone starts a chant, soon picked up by others: 'We're here, we're queer – and we're not going shopping!'

The march has turned down the city's busiest shopping street, a consumer paradise – or nightmare, depending on your point of view. But the chant also contains an ironic reference to the way in which gays have become a target for niche-marketing of consumer goodies. Western, professional, child-free, gay, male couples – with double male earning-power to boot – are a particularly sought-after market.

Sex is for sale and is used to sell products the world over. So, increasingly, is gay sexuality. Even 'gay pride' marches, once so political in nature, are now often conceived as money-spinners – Sydney's annual gay Mardi Gras injects $23 million into the economy.[12]

All of this can be said to reflect a growing social acceptance of minority sexuality that is undoubtedly happening. It's an affirmation, by the market at least, that gay people are 'here and queer' – and welcome to come shopping. And for many people that's enough. Who cares about political rights if you can live a normal life and have your particular consumer needs catered for? If your dollar, pound or yen has as much value and clout as the next straight person's?

The people on this demonstration, clearly, don't think that way.

The market cannot deliver political rights. Nowhere in the world does it do that. If the experience of globalization is anything to go by, quite the opposite is true. The globalized consumer market is by its nature anti-diversity – except in that it wants diverse markets to sell its uniform products to. And multi-national corporations will not stand up for the rights of anyone when the backlash to globalization takes the form of misogyny and homophobia that is costing lives and freedom. Rather, the multinationals will simply try to adjust to the new fundamentalist reality and try and work with it as best it can for maximizing profit.

The lure of the market, the comforts of cultural acceptance, can make the fight for rights and equality seem outdated, unnecessary. Margin has become mainstream to the extent that in some circles there is even talk of a 'post-gay world'.

In his book *The New Gay Teenager* US academic Ritch C Savin-Williams argues that social acceptance is already such that adopting a lesbian or gay political identity is for many young people somewhat passé.

The teenagers he refers to describe themselves in a whole range of sexually diverse ways – 'metrosexual boys', 'bi-anything girls'. Many tick the 'not sure' box when asked about their sexual orientation.

Savin-Williams argues that this is due to the 'normalization of homoeroticism' in a world where pop idols Madonna and Britney Spears may lock lips in public with impunity and shows like *Queer Eye for the Straight Guy* are popular mainstream viewing.

Gay and straight categories may have been fine for their parents, he argues, but not this new generation who are much more relaxed about things.

He quotes a Yale student who says: 'No one really cares or objects to you if you're gay. In fact making a big deal about being gay is seen as distasteful. The unwritten rule is you can do whatever you want as long as you don't act like you're part of an embittered minority.'[9]

This is a view coming from a certain place where battles have been fought and rights won, mainly by previous generations of activists. It is not a situation that is replicated across the US, as many young people fighting against homophobia in that country know only too well. Nor is it a view supported by statistics on the extent of homophobic bullying in US schools (see Chapter 4).

The Revolution that Sylvia Rivera welcomed back in 1969 outside the Stonewall Inn has come in part and for some people. But not for everyone.

For many sexual minority people – living either in conditions of intense persecution or poverty or ignorance about how to protect themselves from AIDS – the issue is plainly one of life or death.

And there can be no doubt about what a politicized sexual identity means to this man writing from Iran, where homosexuality is a capital offence.

'We identify as LGBT people and want the same freedoms as LGBT people world-wide want.'[13]

It's a century and a half since Karl Ulrichs put pen to paper and wrote a defence for his imprisoned friend. But even centuries before that, people who did not fit the heterosexual mold followed their own paths and created their own cultures. The next chapter looks at the hidden histories of some of those people and their societies.

1 *Trans Liberation*, Leslie Feinberg, Beacon Press, 1998. 2 *The Global Emergence of Gay and Lesbian Politics*, Barry D Adam et al eds, Temple University Press, 1999. 3 *The Myth of the Modern Homosexual*, Rictor Norton, Cassell, 1997. 4 *Coming Out*, Jeffrey Weeks, Quartet Books, 1977. 5 'Compulsory Heterosexuality and Lesbian Existence' by Adrienne Rich in *Signs 5*, 1980. 6 *Social Perspectives in Lesbian and Gay Studies*, Peter M Nardi and Beth E Schneider eds, Routledge, 1998. 7 *Female Desires*, Evelyn Blackwood and Saskia E Wieringa eds, Columbia University Press, 1999. 8 *Different Rainbows*, Peter Drucker ed, Gay Men's Press, 2000. 9 *The New Gay Teenager*, Ritch C Savin-Williams, Harvard University Press, 2006. 10 *Reclaiming Genders*, Kate More and Stephen Whittle eds, Cassell, 1999. 11 *Sex, Love and Homophobia*, Vanessa Baird, Amnesty International, 2004. 12 *The Penguin Atlas to Human Sexual Behavior*, Judith Mackay, Penguin 2000. 13 ILGA www.ilga.org/news

# 3 Hidden history

**A global tour of the queer past including... Greeks and Romans... Sufi mystics... Renaissance sodomites... Chinese peach-eaters and vegetarians... Lesbian sailors... transgendered Native Americans... and traditional Africans.**

IT'S A DRINKING party. The topic of conversation turns, as it tends on such occasions, to sex. The comic playwright Aristophanes is telling the others how he thinks all this sex and gender stuff came about.

In the beginning, he says, there were three sexes – male, female and hermaphrodite. Humans looked quite different then. They were round, and had four arms and legs, two faces and two sets of privates.

But because these humans were too powerful and threatened the power of the gods, Zeus split each human down the middle, leaving 'each half with a desperate yearning for the other'.

The man who was a 'slice' of the hermaphrodite sex would naturally be attracted to women, and the woman who was a slice of the hermaphrodite would be drawn to men. But the woman who was a slice of the original female would go for women, just as the man who was a slice of the original male would go for men.

All this takes place in the pages of Plato's *Symposium*. Terms such as 'homosexual' or 'transgender' do not, of course, feature. But what they relate to, as we can see from Aristophanes' story, is as old as the hills.

In some cultures deviations from heterosexuality were deemed quite usual and acceptable. In later, less tolerant times, such evidence was often erased from historical accounts.

Only in the past few decades have queer lives and cultures been considered worthy of serious historical research – in much the way that other 'histories from below' have emerged.

Recovering queer history has not been easy. Much of it went up in flames, quite literally, just like the records of sodomy trials in medieval Europe which were burned together with the convicted.

More still was destroyed by friends and relatives concerned to 'preserve the reputations' of lesbian or gay or bisexual people who had died. Writers and artists who have had evidence of their homosexual desires or relationships destroyed or suppressed in this way include: Edward Lear, Charlotte Bronte, Mary Wollstonecraft, Emily Dickinson, A E Housman, T S Eliot, Ludwig Wittgenstein, George Eliot, Cole Porter, Federico Garcia Lorca and John Donne.[1]

If the history of gay men has been hidden or overlooked, then that of lesbians has been doubly so, on account of both their sexuality and their gender. In some cases anthropological information dating back several decades remained unpublished because the anthropologists feared damaging their reputations.

That has changed now, thanks largely to lesbian scholarship. Lesbian traditions have been found among rich Muslim women in Mombasa, Kenya; the vegetarian sisterhoods of pre-Revolutionary China; the women-marrying-women traditions in Ghana, Lesotho and other African countries; and same-sex relationships between cousins in Aboriginal Australian communities, to name but a few.[2]

Meanwhile, biographers have dug into the history of specific women such as Britain's Queen Anne who had a long-term relationship with her lady-in-waiting Sarah Churchill; the Spanish socialite Mercedes De Acosta who counted both Marlene Dietrich and Greta Garbo among her lovers; and Eve Balfour, born in 1898, founder of both the Soil Association and the modern organic farming movement.[3]

Back in 1953 gay Beat poet Jack Spicer wrote: 'We homosexuals are the only minority group that completely lacks any vestige of a separate cultural heritage.'

Today, this is no longer the case. The following are a few items from the ever-expanding site of sexual minority history.

### Greek love and Roman decorum

So obvious is homosexuality in the culture of Ancient Greece that it has been impossible for prudish later civilizations to entirely conceal.

Classical art and religion abounds with references to same-sex love. Zeus himself is shown to be bisexual in his pursuit of the beautiful youth Ganymede. In Greek literature and philosophy the suggestion is that such sexualities are commonplace and accepted behavior. It's just a question of preference, not morals.

Given the low position of women in Ancient Greek society it is perhaps not surprising that sex between women barely gets a mention. Sappho, the lyric poet of Lesbos, has fired imaginations and given her name to much, but we know precious little about her. She probably lived between 620 and 550 BC, ran a school for young ladies and wrote erotic verse addressed to a woman or various women.

Translations of a later Greek physician Soranos,

---

### Sexual decorum in Rome

For the free adult male citizen of Ancient Rome two sexual roles were deemed decorous: irrumo – to offer the penis for sucking – and futuo, to penetrate a female or pedico, to penetrate a male. Indecorous roles for male citizens, but permissible to anyone else, were: fello, to fellate, and ceveo, which, according to historian David Halperin, is not translatable into English.[4] Legal prostitution, both male and female, thrived in Rome and prostitutes were defined by what they offered. A youthful passive male was called a catamitus. A constant companion would be called a concubinus. Exoleti – usually slaves – offered a wide range of practices. Male prostitutes with especially large genitals were known as dauci, and would gain custom from both women and men. ■

---

who practiced in Rome in the second century AD, refer to women called *tribades*. Soranos says: 'These practice both kinds of sex, but are more eager to have sexual intercourse with women than with men and pursue women with an almost masculine jealousy.'[4]

More important in highly patriarchal Greek and Roman society was not the gender of the person a male might sleep with but the role and power dynamic within the relationship. For example Artemeidorus Daldianus, writing in the second century AD, says: 'For a man to be penetrated by a richer and older man is good: for it is customary to receive from such men. To be penetrated by a younger and poorer is bad: for it is the custom to give to such a person.'

Not only was same-sex sex acceptable – it might also be considered aesthetically and emotionally desirable. Plutarch in his *Dialogue on Love* asserts that 'the noble lover engages in love wherever he sees excellence and splendid natural endowment without regard to any difference in physiological detail. The lover of human beauty [will] be fairly and equably disposed towards both sexes, instead of supposing that males and females are as different in the matter of love as they are in their clothes.'[4]

## Islamic passions

Given current Muslim fundamentalist attitudes towards homosexuality, it is perhaps surprising to find in medieval Islam a flourishing literature of homosexual eroticism.

'It's probably fair to say,' writes historian John Boswell, 'that this is more than a literary convention.'

When Saadia Gaon, a Jew living in 10th-century Muslim society, discusses the desirability of 'passionate love' he apparently refers only to homosexual passion. Homosexuals are frequently and neutrally mentioned in classical Arabic writings as a distinct type of human being. Three debates on the preference of homosexual or heterosexual love occur in *The*

*Thousand and One Nights*, a classic of Arabic literature. In tale 419, a woman observes a man staring longingly at some boys and remarks to him: 'I perceive you are among those who prefer men to women.'

A ninth-century text of human psychology by Qustã ibn Luqã treats 20 areas in which humans may be distinguished psychologically. One area is sexual object choice. Some men, Qustã explains, are 'disposed towards' women, some towards other men, and some towards both. Qustã believed that homosexuality was often inherited, as did ar-Razi and many other Muslim scientific writers.[4]

The invasion of Muslims into Spain in 711 canceled repressive Christian laws against homosexuality which demanded castration, head-shaving, whipping and banishment as punishment. Muslim rule, which lasted 700 years throughout southern Spain, fostered an era of far greater intellectual, religious and sexual tolerance.[5]

Poets from the Sufi mystic tradition, in particular, focused on forms of transgendered and homoerotic behavior. It is this tradition which has inspired what is regarded as some of the most beautiful male love poetry in world literature, including the work of Jalal Al Din Rumi (1207-1273). There are a number of secular texts regarding homoerotic love, influenced by Sufism. One such is *Qabus-nama* by Kai-Ka us ibn Iskandar, an 11th-century emir who urges his son to fall in love and to be bisexual so that he can enjoy the pleasures of other males as well as women.[6]

**Painters, printers and gondoliers**
Renaissance Europe saw, paradoxically, both extreme punishments for homosexuality and wide practice of it.

Noblemen often had their same-sex favorites – France's Henri III and England's James I were notorious, while England's Earl of Rochester famously wrote: 'missing my whore I bugger my page'. Men right across the social spectrum had sex with each other, be they London merchants and actors, Venetian barber-surgeons and gondolieri, Genevan printers, laborers, servants or sailors.

The apprenticeship system was especially conducive as apprentices lived with their masters. The painter Donatello was only one of many painters believed to choose his disciples 'more for beauty than talent'. The Siennese artist Giantantonio Bazzi, insisted he be publicly referred to by his nickname *Il Sodomi* ('the sodomite'). Michelangelo's neo-platonic passion for several men was widely known, though he insisted on his pious celibacy. Leonardo da Vinci too was accused of sodomy. And when Benvenuto Cellini was called a 'dirty sodomite' by a rival, he countered with: 'I wish to God I did know how to indulge in such a noble practice; after all, we read that Jove [Zeus] enjoyed it with Ganymede in paradise.'

Women are less well documented, but Pierre de Bourdeille reports from the 16th-century French court that 'after the fashion was brought from Italy by a lady of quality who I will not name', sexual relations between women had become very common. Some of these were young girls and widows who preferred to make love to each other than 'to go to a man and thus become pregnant and lose their honor or their virginity'. Others were women who used other women to enhance their love-making with men 'because this little exercise, as I have heard say, is nothing but an apprenticeship to come for the greater [love] of men'. For him, as for many men of his time, the attraction of women for each other was not to be taken as a serious threat to their own access to women's sexual favors.[4]

There are reliable 17th century accounts of Queen Christina of Sweden, who abdicated in order not to marry. Other accounts show women of various classes and social backgrounds having sex with women: a lady-in-waiting to the Duchess of York, a French actress, two wives in New World Plymouth found 'engaged in lewd behavior together... upon a bed'. And there's the curious case of Italian Sister Benedetta Carlini, sentenced to life imprisonment for blasphemy after claiming to have had visions that required her cell-mate to make love to her.[6]

## Two-spirit Native Americans

Same-sex and transgender traditions were prevalent in most Native American societies. There are reports of both women and men living in same-sex marriages, of women who dressed and acted as men and men who acted and dressed as women.

The European chroniclers who first came across such customs described them in terms that belonged to their own world. American Indian homosexual men were called *berdaches* – French for 'slave-boys', used to refer to passive male homosexuals. The name stuck – although its servile connotations were quite inappropriate and the term 'Two-Spirit' is now preferred by some.

Gay transvestites were often the shamans or healers of the tribe. Sometimes they had specific religious duties and were regarded as having special intellectual, artistic and spiritual qualities. The ability to combine female and male qualities often put them into the role of mediators between the sexes.[7]

It was relatively easy for women in North American Indian societies to take traditionally male roles and live as men. Girls in the Yukon who declined marriage and child-bearing would dress as men and take part in hunting expeditions. This was also true of Sioux women who became warriors and married women. In the Kaska Indian families of Canada, parents would raise one of their daughters to become a warrior. Her sexual experiences would be with other women. Indeed, if there was sexual contact with a man it would ruin the lesbian's luck with game.

A 19th-century army officer who studied American Indian customs closely, reported on male pairs, saying: 'They really seem to fall in love with men and I have known this affectionate interest to live for years.' The union of two men was often publicly recognized in a 'friendship dance'. Historian Walter M Williams argues that such friendships were not necessarily homosexual, but that for all males who felt erotic attraction to other men, these relationships provided a natural avenue for same-sex behavior.

Indian society did not conceive of the universe as being composed of absolutes and polarities of black and white, male and female, good and evil. Nor did it automatically equate gender identity and sex roles with biological sex characteristics. Similarly, the spiritual and the physical were not separate. An understanding of the spiritual informed a group's every institution, custom, endeavor and pastime. What was 'natural' to a person was what the spirits told that person to be. So, if the spirits told someone, through visions or dreams, to act and dress as a person of the opposite sex, for that person not to do so would be to go against their culture and to endanger their own lives. Or in the words of one Indian elder: 'To us a man is what nature or his dreams make him. We accept him for what he wants to be.'[3]

Today gay and transgendered people of Native American descent are drawing encouragement from their recovered history. Gary Bowen, of Apache and Scotch-Irish descent, for example says: 'My own transgendered state is a sacred calling given to me by the Spirit, not a neurosis discovered by white medicine. As a person of Native descent I look to my ancestors for guidance in these matters.'[8]

**'Sharing the peach' and vegetarian sisterhoods in China**
Homosexuality has a long and documented history in China. The third century BC text, *Chronicles of the*

*Warring States*, for example, includes numerous biographies of major figures of the period that make plain their homosexuality.

From the *Chronicles* we know about the affection between Duke Ling of Wei and his minister, Ni Xia. Once, when the two men were taking a stroll in an orchard, Ni picked a peach off a tree and took a bite of it. The fruit was so delicious that he offered the rest of it to the duke; a common euphemism for male homosexual love, 'the love of shared peach', is derived from this account.

Later official histories too did not hide the fact of the homosexual orientation of key historical personages, writes historian Vivien W Ng. We learn from the *History of the Former Han* that the last Emperor Aidid (who ruled from 6-1 BC) had a number of male lovers, and that he was especially fond of one of them, Dong Xian. One day, as the two men were napping together on a couch, with Dong's head resting on the Emperor's sleeve, the latter was called away to grant an audience. He cut off the sleeve rather than awaken his beloved. From this episode is derived another common literary term for homosexual love, *duanxiu*, 'the cut sleeve'.

It appears that male homosexuality was tolerated as long as it was not an exclusive sexual expression and that men fulfilled their procreative duties. In the 17th century homoerotic literature came into its own and flourished in China.

Writer Shen Defu noted that male homosexuality was commonplace in the province of Fujian: 'The Fujianese especially favor male homosexuality. The preference is not limited to any particular social or economic class... They call each other 'bond brothers'. When the elder bond brother enters the house of the younger brother, he is welcomed and loved by the parents as one would a son-in-law...'

Most of the homoerotic literature celebrated male

relations. There was one notable exception, though – Li Yu's play *Pitying the Fragrant Companion* which is the story of two women (one married, one a Buddhist nun) who love each other so much they perform a wedding ceremony for themselves. The married woman successfully conspires to have her husband accept her lover as a concubine and the two women live happily ever after.[4]

### Women who passed as men

In early modern Europe, there are a number of instances of women who dressed as men and passed themselves off as such.

There could be many motives. Some did it to become soldiers or sailors; some for safety when traveling; some to gain access to male power and freedom. Others did it to pursue other women, whom they might even marry. And sometimes these wives claimed not to know that their husbands were a little different from what might be expected.

## The curious case of Maria van Antwerpen

The case of Maria van Antwerpen is one of the best recorded; it created quite a sensation in her own time. On 23 February 1769 she was convicted by the court of the Dutch city of Gouda for 'gross and excessive fraud in changing her name and quality' and 'mocking holy and human laws concerning marriage'.

● Eight years earlier she had dressed herself in men's clothing and enlisted as a soldier. In this disguise, she courted and married a woman – without the latter realizing Maria's sex. And it was not the first time Maria had done this.

● At her trial Maria said she was 'not like any other woman and therefore it was best to dress in man's clothing'. She said she had 'the appearance of a woman' but in nature was a man.

● She recalled meeting a girl who had fallen into prostitution. This had made Maria realize, she said, of the fate that awaited her unless she donned men's clothes and took up arms.

● By 1800 increasing bureaucracy made it harder for women like Maria to live as men. Military service was enforced, all conscripts had to undergo medical examinations, and it became difficult to travel without identification papers.

● In her autobiography the resourceful Maria said: 'It often made me wrathful that Mother Nature treated me with so little compassion against my inclinations and the passions of my heart.'[9] ∎

If caught, women who cross-dressed could be severely punished, executed even. The main crime they were thought to have committed was not lesbianism, but fraud – for impersonating a man and assuming male social power.

Researchers Lotte van de Pol and Rudolf Dekker have discovered 119 cases in the Netherlands during the 17th and 18th centuries and an equal number in England. Denmark, Spain and Italy had other recorded cases. They reckon this is probably the tip of an iceberg.[9]

For women who were adventurous or destitute or had fallen on bad times, passing oneself off as a man was a good option. Popular songs recounted adventures of female sailors and soldiers, and even though they were mostly derisive some told of heroism and rewards for bravery. In 1762 an Englishman jestingly wrote that there were so many disguised women in the army that it would be better to create a separate regiments for them.

## African traditions

A number of contemporary African leaders have made public statements to the effect that homosexuality is not part of African tradition. Both anthropologists and historians have found otherwise. Same-sex eroticism and transgender behavior were apparently known to Africans long before Africa – with perhaps the exception of Egypt and Libya – was subjected to non-African influences.

Among Azande people, living in what is today south-western Sudan, northern D R Congo, and the south-eastern corner of the Central African Republic, a form of intergenerational homoeroticism was practiced from long ago until the beginning of the 20th century.

Anthropologist Edward Evans-Pritchard insisted that this and other forms of same-sex eroticism were indigenous and not the result of foreign influence. The typical relationship was between a ruler or warrior and a younger male.

Azande women also practiced same-sex eroticism, although this activity was apparently feared by most men as it was thought to double women's power. Lesbianism seems to have been especially common among women living in the courts of princes. Using a dildo fashioned from a root was popular. Lesbianism also had magical associations. Lovemaking between women, it was imagined, led to the birth of 'the cat-people'.

Transgendered homosexuality is documented among the Nuba peoples of Nilotic Sudan. They have various names for men engaging in same-sex eroticism, and even same-sex marriages occur, according to anthropologist S F Nadel. Homosexual or transgendered males have had a role as spiritual functionaries among a number of African cultures – the Lango people of Uganda, Murus of Kenya, Ilas of southern Zambia and Zulu people of South Africa.

The Yoruba religion of Nigeria had the widest dispersal of all African religions. Many of the 12 million Africans who arrived in the Americas between the early 16th and the late 19th centuries were of Yoruba ancestry. Their religion – also known as the 'way of the Orisha' – has carved out a niche for sexual minority people. More than 25 terms, most of African origin, are employed to describe such persons. These include adodi, which may be applied to homosexual, bisexual or transgendered males and alakuata, which may be applied to lesbian, bisexual or transgendered women.

This is the Yoruba religion primarily as it is practiced in the Americas.[6] In most of the African countries mentioned above homosexuality is illegal – in Sudan, home of Azandes, the death penalty applies. The laws used are either Islamic *shari'a* or old British colonial rules.

## A sense of continuity

Queer histories help gay and transgender people to discover and recover a sense of culture and continuity. Through her own historical explorations Afro-American author Audre Lorde was able to connect her sexuality with the zami of the Caribbean culture of her parents and also the same-sex unions between women in Africa.

Rather than 'looking for the homosexual in history', recent queer scholarship has tended to focus more on the way in which hetero-normative frameworks have been imposed on societies, often to consolidate religious or imperial power, which had the result of narrowing down sexuality.[10]

Whichever form it takes, queer history has helped make connecting paths through experience that has too often been suppressed, broken and silenced by homophobia – which is what the next chapter is about.

**1** *The Myth of the Modern Homosexual*, Rictor Norton, Cassell, 1999. **2** *Female Desires*, Evelyn Blackwood and Saskia Wieringa eds, Columbia University Press, 1999. **3** *Portraits to the Wall*, Rose Collis, Cassell, 1994. **4** *Hidden from History*, Martin Bauml Duberman, Martha Vicinus, George Chauncey eds, Penguin, 1989. **5** *Homophobia*, Byrne Fone, Metropolitan Books, 2000. **6** Cassell's *Encyclopedia of Queer Myth, Symbol and Spirit*, Randy P Conner, David Hatfield Sparks, Mariya Sparks eds, 1997. **7** 'What your dreams make you', Rae Trewartha, New Internationalist, November 1989. **8** *Trans Liberation*, Leslie Feinberg, Beacon Press, 1998. **9** *The Tradition of Female Transvestism in Early Modern Europe*, Lotte C van de Pol and Rudolf M Dekker, Macmillan Press, 1989. **10** *Gay Life and Culture: A World History*, Robert Aldrich ed., Thames and Hudson, 2006

# 4 Homophobia – roots and shoots

**Millennia of hatred... Christian fires... Aztec punishments... Imperial edicts... Manchu control-freaks... to Siberia without love... the Nazi holocaust... McCarthy's witch-trials... Castro's boats... fundamentalist furies... African panic... Middle East aflame... youth in peril.**

'IF ONE CONSIDERS how fearfully damaging sodomy is for the state and how much this disgusting vice spreads secretly, the death penalty does not seem hard.'

These are the words of Johann Michaelis, a German Protestant theologian who lived in the 18th century. But they could have been said in many other places, and at many other times, including our own.

Hundreds of thousands have paid with their lives for breaking the sexual rules of their societies. But the punishments meted out for homosexual behavior have often been accompanied by a particular virulence, an extreme reaction we now term 'homophobia'.

It's a relatively new word, emerging in the 1960s. In 1972, George Weinberg's book *Society and the Healthy Homosexual* defined it as 'the dread of being at close quarters with homosexuals'. Mark Freedman added to the definition a description of homophobia as 'extreme rage and fear reaction to homosexuals'.[1] And writer Audre Lorde added greater depth in 1978 when she defined homophobia as 'fear of feelings of love for members of one's own sex and therefore hatred of those feelings in others'.

## Plagues, quakes and famines

In the Greek and Roman pre-Christian era there were no laws against same-sex sex and no punishments. But between 100 BC and 400 AD attitudes towards homosexuality changed in Europe and the Middle

East. In late Antiquity what had been viewed as the highest form of love was being seen less favorably. Asceticism was on the increase, derived partly from the anti-sexual arguments of Neo-Platonists and Jewish philosophers and from the doctrines of the new Christian sects who were clamoring against 'pagan ways'. Judaic and early Christian writing showed a more general aversion to homosexual behavior and cross-dressing – a view propagated most famously by the Apostle Paul (see Chapter 6).

Nonetheless, homosexuality flourished in some early Christian communities. Writing about the community in Antioch, Greek church father John Chrysostom complained: 'This outrage is perpetrated with the utmost openness. Far from being ashamed they take pride in their activities and in the middle of cities men do unseemly things to each other, just as if they were in a vast desert.'

In 313 AD the Roman Emperor Constantine declared the empire Christian and a 342 AD edict mandated 'exquisite punishment' for men who offered themselves in a 'womanly fashion' to other men. In 390 AD homosexuality was made illegal and the Church declared that such acts were sinful because they were 'unnatural'.

It was the Byzantine Emperor Justinian who made homosexual acts punishable by death in 533 AD. By now homosexuality (and blasphemy) were being blamed for natural disasters such as famines, earthquakes and pestilence. The Gothic peoples that succeeded Rome and converted to Roman Christianity were no more tolerant. A law of 650 AD in Visigothic Spain refers to it as a 'crime that ought always to be detested' and 'an execrable moral depravity'.[1]

### Age of faith, age of sodomy

At the beginning of the millennium the Church began to centralize its power in the person of the Pope. As part of this process it codified the doctrines and laws of the past thousand years.

This enabled the Church to designate more clearly who was the enemy of the faith. Heretics and those whose sexual practices were deemed contrary to the dictates of natural law began to be classified and persecuted.

Emboldened by the Crusades, the papacy sought to extend its religious authority over nations and monarchs as well as over spiritual lives. To do this it would have to be morally unassailable. But many of its priests were married and some kept concubines, even boys. Anticlerical feeling was strong and the moral authority of the Church was weak.

In a drive to increase the Church's prestige and therefore power, reformers focused on 'sodomy' as the emblem of the sickness afflicting the church. Historian Byrne Fone comments that at this time the Church began to 'conflate sexual with doctrinal deviance, sodomy with heresy,' and that 'all manner of religiously unorthodox, the politically suspect, and the simply foreign – Muslims, Jews, heretics – were routinely accused of sexual crimes, among them sodomy'.

Accusations of sodomy were used as a political weapon against enemies. At the beginning of the 13th century, Pope Innocent III decreed that convicted her-

---

## Li livres di jostice et de plet

Intolerance of sexual deviation grew throughout the 13th century and was reflected in literary texts and horrific depictions of the sodomite. The earliest legal reference to lesbians appears to be the 1207 French law code Li livres di jostice et de plet which prescribed that a man who engages in homosexual relations shall, on a first offense, lose his testicles; on a second offense lose his member (penis); and shall be burned to death on the third offense; and that a woman shall, somewhat confusingly, 'lose her member each time and on the third must be burned'. ■

From *Homophobia*, Byrne Fone, Metropolitan, 2000.

etics should forfeit their property and be put to death. These edicts justified the bloody campaign to wipe out the Albigensian (or Cathar) heresy, which cost the lives of thousands in south-eastern France in 1208.

How many people were actually executed for sodomy between the 10th and the 13th century is not known. This is partly because sentences often condemned the sodomite to be burned together with the records of his trial, the crime being 'so hideous it could not be named'.

## Officers of the Night

In its cultural expressions, the Renaissance abounded in same-sex love. But this was accompanied by repression even more ferocious. The 14th and 15th centuries saw a European panic over homosexuality.

In the Italian city of Sienna the governing council appointed special Officers of the Night 'to ensure true peace and maintain good morals' by pursuing sodomites and bringing them to trial. In Florence, youths under 14 who willingly submitted to homosexual advances were driven naked from the city; others were castrated. Investigations were conducted in secret; anyone might denounce anyone. Torture was used to extract confessions.

The convicted would be displayed on the pillory, to be abused and beaten by righteous citizens. If they survived this ordeal, the next stage was to be burned at the stake. Any site where sodomy was supposed to have been performed was deemed to be polluted. Even referring to sodomy was actionable – a fine was imposed for singing or writing songs that mentioned it. But it appears that sodomy was rampant nonetheless. In Florence, Officers of the Night tried some 15,000 men and boys and convicted over 2,000 between 1432 and 1502.

St Bernadino of Sienna was to write: 'I have heard of boys who dress themselves up and go around boasting of their sodomizers, and they make a practice of it for pay and go about encouraging others to this ugly sin.' Bernadino argued that sodomy caused plague and sodomizers actively spread poison through the city.

In England, in 1533, came the first piece of homophobic secular legislation of the English-speaking world. An act passed by Henry VIII brought sodomy within the purview of statute law. This law made buggery punishable by death, and did not mention women.[2]

A statute passed the previous year by the Holy Roman Emperor Charles V of Spain did include women and condemned both sexes to death by burning. A later law, in 1574, noted: 'If a woman commits this vice or sin against nature, she shall be fastened naked to a stake in the Street of Locusts, shall remain there all day and all night under reliable guard, and the following day be burned outside the city.'[2]

Records from Barcelona, Valencia and Saragossa show 1,600 convictions between 1560 and 1640. Waves of persecution often followed certain disruptive events. In Seville, for example, food shortages in 1580, the forced resettlement of Spanish Muslims to the city in 1585, and an epidemic of plague in 1600, were all followed by the rounding up of presumed sodomites.

Protestant attitudes to same-sex relations were no different. In Geneva, Switzerland, where John Calvin had in 1541 established a strict Protestant theocracy, the authorities kept careful records of sodomy trials. In 1555 the numbers rose, paralleling the trend across Europe.

### Empires of hatred

Meanwhile in the Americas the Europeans had arrived – and with them the will to conquer native peoples and subject them to European religion and customs, including homophobia.

They did not waste time. In October 1513 the Spanish conquistador Vasco Nunez de Balboa ordered the massacre of several hundred Panamanian Indians in the village of Quarequa, 40 of whom had, he was sure, engaged in sodomy.

One account relates how Balboa went to the house of the king and found 'young men in woman's apparel, smooth and effeminately decked'. He commanded that they be thrown to his dogs. A 1594 engraving shows naked victims writhing on the ground as dogs tear them apart.

Similarly, conquistador Hernan Cortéz believed that the great Aztec civilization upon which he had stumbled in Mexico was rife with sodomy: 'We have been informed, and are most certain it is true, that they are all sodomites and practice that abominable sin.'

However, Latin American scholars looking into gay history have found that while there is evidence of tolerance to same-sex relations in Zapotec society, this does not appear to be the case among the Aztecs. According to Mexican writer Max Mejia, the Aztecs had very harsh laws against sodomy, punishing it with public execution. This mainly applied to men but women were not exempt.[3]

Mejia describes the city of Texcoco under King Nezahualcoyotzin, where 'the infamous sin was punished with immense rigor, since the individual, tied to a stick, was covered by all the boys of the city with ash, so that he was buried in it, while his entrails were removed through the sexual area, and then he was buried in ash'.

Punishment for sodomy was meted out mostly to men or women who cross-dressed. Spanish Friar Bartolomé de las Casas noted that: 'The man who dressed as woman and the woman found dressed with men's clothes, died because of this.'

However, there were exceptions. The practice was tolerated when it took place in religious rituals. Members of the spiritual élite escaped punishment because of their divine ordination and their relationship to the god. Elsewhere in the region, Europeans

were seeking and finding sodomy. One Spanish conquistador asserted that the Caribs 'were sodomites
more than any other race'.[1]

Further North, Spanish, French and English explor-
ers were noticing the cross-dressing traditions of the
Native American cultures (see Chapter 3). Many commentators expressed their abhorrence at what they
saw among Iroquois people, the Sioux and others.

In North America, Puritan settlers were terrified
that the 'New Jerusalem' they sought to create would
become a 'New Sodom'. It was not just the customs
of the indigenous people that concerned them, but
sodomy within their own ranks too. In 1629 five
'sodomitical boys' were shipped back to England for
punishment, presumably by hanging. In 1636 the
Plymouth Colony drew up a code of laws in which the
crime of sodomy was punishable by death.

American preacher Samuel Whiting sermonized in
1666: 'When men commit filthiness with men and
women with women... this makes them ripe for ruin.
Strange lusts bring strange punishments; strange fire
kindled upon earth, brings strange fire from heaven.
Fire naturally ascends but the fire that destroyed
Sodom descended...'

In most of the colonies English laws of punishment
by death were considered to be in force. Puritan settlers
in New England made lesbianism a capital crime in the
mid-17th century but there are no known prosecutions.

### A threat to the state

On the other side of the world, in late imperial China,
an era of tolerance towards homosexuality was coming to an end for a different reason: the arrival of the
Manchus in 1644 and the creation of a new Qing/
Ch'ing dynasty. Using principles of Confucianism
the Manchus imposed the 'rectification of names' – a
process by which each person was to know their role
and perform it accordingly. Historian Vivien W Ng

notes: 'Very early on the Qing Government recognized that law codes were a powerful symbol of the authority of the state. They insisted that men must be good husbands and women good wives – deviation from these prescribed roles would not be tolerated. Seen in this light, homosexuality was a violation of the principle of rectification of names.' But homosexuality persisted and in 1740 a law was finally passed making sodomy a crime. A survey of trial cases shows that the Qing Government was less forgiving of male homosexuals than of women, maybe because names were passed through men and it was a filial and patriarchal duty to sire sons.

In Europe, too, during this period sodomites were perceived as a danger to the state. German Protestant theologian Johann Michaelis declared that homosexuality led to depopulation, weakened marriage and 'brings the nation to the brink of destruction...'

In Protestant England and Holland 'reform societies' tried to clamp down on a growing gay subculture found in so-called 'molly' houses where gay men could meet. In Holland between 1730 and 1731, 60 males were executed, many of them in their teens. In England entrapment of homosexuals by police and their spies became common. While the rest of Europe came under the influence of revolutionary ideas and the French decriminalization of homosexuality in 1791, in England persecution increased. In spite of pleas for reason and tolerance from the likes of philosopher Jeremy Bentham, hangings continued well into the 19th century. Between 1806 and 1836, 60 men were hanged for sodomy and Britain was the last European country to abandon the death penalty for this offense in 1861.

In the mid 19th century laws against homosexuality were applied in the colonies of the British Empire, including India. This was part of a colonial drive to clamp down on any local traditions of sexual diversity. In India the position of transgendered hijras – a traditional caste of eunuchs with a 2,000-year history – began to lose its legitimacy. The British refused to lend legal support to the hijras' traditional right to beg or extort money, hoping in this way to discourage 'the abominable practices of the wretches'. In some states the British criminalized emasculation, aimed specifically at the *hijras*.[4]

British homophobic attitudes were to persist in its colonies during and after the struggle for independence. From the 1920s to the 1940s there was a campaign (led, unfortunately, by Mahatma Gandhi) to erase all positive references to transgenderism and same-sex desire in Indian, especially Hindu, culture. During these years, Gandhi sent out squads of his devotees to destroy the erotic representations, especially homoerotic and lesbian ones, carved into Hindu temples dating from the 11th century.[5]

Writer and philosopher Rabindranath Tagore was able to halt this violent action. Nevertheless the campaign to erase the history of gender and sexual variance was continued by Prime Minister Jawaharlal Nehru, who held office from 1946 to 1964. Like Gandhi, he had been educated in England, and like him, he wished to convey the message that it was the English who had brought homosexuality to India. He was upset when his friend Alain Danielou published photographs of traditional Hindu sculptures depicting homoeroticism and transgender people.

Australia and Aotearoa/New Zealand also inherited British attitudes and laws against homosexuality. In Australia these were to persist until decriminalization started in 1972 (to be completed 25 years later with Tasmania the last state to change its laws). In Aotearoa/New Zealand legality came in 1986. But the countries with some of the longest prison sentences are former colonies in Africa and Asia that still cling to the old British laws (see Appendix).

**Fascist war against 'sexual degenerates'**

The 1914-18 world war brought in its wake a revolution in social attitudes, especially in relation to gender and sexuality. Women gained the vote in many parts of Europe. Freud's psychoanalytic theories were getting people to think differently about sex and sexuality.

Sexology became a field of academic research, especially in Germany. By the 1920s Berlin was the center for such investigation – especially the Institute of Sexology created by Magnus Hirschfeld, a leading light in the World League for Sexual Reform. The city also had a flourishing gay culture.

All that came to an abrupt end when Hitler came to power in 1933. The Nationalist Socialist (Nazi) Party had already made its position clear in 1928 when it declared: 'Those who are considering love between men or between women are our enemies.'[2]

Within the first year of Hitler's rule homosexuals, transvestites, pimps and other 'sexual degenerates' were being rounded up. Some 50,000 officially defined homosexuals were imprisoned. An estimated 15,000 were to perish in concentration camps.[2,6]

Homosexuals were usually near the bottom of the prison hierarchy. They were subject to humiliation, singled out for special tortures and dangerous work. Most did not survive. The general policy was to work them to death, but they were also subjected to medical experimentation. In 1944 a series of experiments aimed at the elimination of homosexuality were started in Buchenwald Camp.

According to researcher Erwin J Haeberle, the Nazis – with their policy of stigmatization, imprisonment and medical treatment – continued and intensified what had been general practice in many societies.

What happened after the war is instructive. Nazi policies towards homosexuals were ignored and neglected by researchers. Little was published on the matter for several decades. The whole subject was distasteful to Germans and Allies alike. After all, male homosexuality was still a crime in Britain, the US, both East and West Germany and the USSR. Thus the homosexual inmates of concentration camps were not considered unjustly imprisoned and therefore could remain uncompensated for their suffering.[2,6] Not only that, they could be re-imprisoned. Only in the late 1960s did the two Germanys reform their anti-sodomy laws. An emerging gay-rights movement in the 1970s 'discovered' the Nazi persecution of homosexuals.

In General Franco's fascist Spain there was, following the bloody 1936-39 Civil War, a return to traditional Spanish values. Family, Catholicism and patriotism were the elements that held together the dictatorship – plus a traditional hostility to homosexuality. The most famous victim to Falangist homophobic violence was the poet Federico Garcia Lorca. Homosexuals were prosecuted under various laws: 'public scandal', 'vagrancy and villainy' – and imprisoned. A center for the rehabilitation of homosexuals used aversion therapies (electroshock, emetics) but the regime settled for creating an atmosphere of silence and denial rather than overt persecution of gays and lesbians. Only after Franco's death did a gay and lesbian movement begin to emerge.[7]

## 'Imperialist relics'

In Russia there was a brief flowering of gay culture, literature and politics between the 1905 Revolution and the February Revolution of 1917. But by the 1920s this had already withered. Critically, the idea of rights for homosexuals never got the support of either Lenin or Trotsky. The new Soviet regime saw homosexuality as an illness to be cured.

In 1923 the People's Commisariat of Public Health declared: 'Science has now established, with precision that excludes all doubt, [that homosexuality] is not ill-will or crime but sickness'. A so-called 'expert' on homosexuality, Mark Sereisky, described experiments to try and cure homosexuality by transplanting a heterosexual male's testicle into a homosexual.[2]

Homosexuality was mentioned less and less in Soviet literature and by 1930 was barely mentioned at all. The works of established lesbian and gay writers and poets were systematically ignored – or interpreted to gloss over their homosexual content. Gays within the Party were urged to commit themselves to psychiatric clinics. Even the great socialist filmmaker Sergei Eisenstein was blackmailed by the Soviet Government and forced to go through a show marriage.

The growing hostility towards homosexuality culminated in a law in 1933 which was extended to all soviet republics in 1934. This banned sexual relations between men and prescribed five years hard labor as punishment. Author Maxim Gorky writing in *Pravda* and *Izvestia* called it 'a triumph of proletarian humanitarianism' and wrote that legalization of homosexuality had been the main cause of Fascism. Persecuting gays had become part of the Communist catechism.

The Soviet law did not just make homosexuality a crime against public morality – it was now seen as a crime against the State, along with banditry, counter-revolutionary activities, sabotage and espionage. In 1936 Commissar Justice Nikolai Rylenko proclaimed that there was no reason for anyone to be homosexual after two decades of socialism and anyone persisting in being so must be 'remnants of the exploiting classes'.

In practice, Maoist China was more hostile still. After the 1949 Revolution Chinese gays were rounded up and shot. Lesbians belonging to women-only sisterhoods fled into exile. Homosexuality was declared officially 'non-existent'. In later decades homosexual acts were condemned under 'hooliganism' laws. Presumably no specific laws could pertain to something that officially did not exist. For most of the 20th century the Stalinist and Maoist currents that dominated the international anti-capitalist Left fostered anti-gay prejudice. In the Cuban Revolution's first years the Soviet-linked United Party of the Socialist Cuban Revolution actively promoted prejudice. Castro denounced homosexuality as a hangover from the corrupt Batista era; it had to be eradicated by revolutionary puritanism. Gays were incarcerated in rehabilitation camps during the 1960s and then expelled as part of the mass 'Mariel' exodus of 'social undesirables' from Cuba to the US in 1983. At best, homosexuality was seen as an imperialist relic – at worst a gross social degeneration.[8]

### 'As dangerous as communists'

In the mid-20th century, the US view that homosexuality was a sickness started to go into overdrive. During the Second World War gays in the US army were discharged into military psychiatric wards where they were used in developing new techniques for identifying homosexuals. A study of 1,400 patients at one hospital observed that homosexuals did not show a 'gag reflex' when a tongue depressor was put down their throat. This 'gag reflex', the study concluded, 'is a definite aid in screening candidates not only for the military services, but for positions where the sexual deviant must be eliminated'. The military identification of homosexuals set the precedent for the massive screening that was to follow after the War.[2]

'Treatment' ranged from hypnotherapy, electro-convulsive and emetic aversion therapies, and surgery. Until the 1950s hysterectomies, hormone injections and clitoridectomies were performed on lesbians in the US.[9]

But psychiatry became the weapon of choice. *Newsweek* in 1949 urged that the 'degenerate' may be 'brought to the realization of the error of their ways by psychiatry'. Between 1950 and 1955 the US Government investigated its own employees, members of the armed forces and others in an attempt to discover communist agents and sympathizers. One aspect of the investigation was to attempt to link political beliefs with sexual activities, and many suspected of being communist were also accused of being homosexual. The notion of homosexuality as a political menace was established. In 1950 *The New York Times* was reporting that 'sexual perverts have infiltrated our government in recent years' and were 'perhaps as dangerous as actual communists'.

The US Senate Committee produced a report in 1950 saying that: 'The lack of emotional stability which is found in most sex perverts and the weakness of their moral fiber makes them susceptible to the blandishments offered by espionage agents and easy prey to blackmailers.' Homosexuals came under scrutiny to a greater extent under the McCarthy 'witch trials'. By January 1955 more than 8,000 people had been removed from government jobs as a security risk; more than 600 were found to be 'sexual perverts'.[1] Paradoxically these trials in the 1950s – to root out 'communists' and other 'subversives' – helped to spur the creation of the modern homosexual-rights movement in the US.

### 'Finish them off'

During the spate of military dictatorships that beset Latin America during the 1970s and 1980s, homophobia increased. In Chile setting up lesbian or gay groups was defined by law as an act of terrorism because it 'attacks the family'. In Brazil, gays were not specifically targeted by the military but the general clamp-down on literary and artistic expression discouraged gays on the streets (except during Carnival!) and prevented the formation of a movement.

In Argentina the targeting of gays was very explicit. After the March 1976 military coup, gay activists were tortured and murdered. Others went into exile. The rest ceased their public activities and the movement was dissolved. This was to be the case during most of Argentina's years of brutal dictatorship. But then, in 1982, a few groups began to organize again. The dictatorship – then on its last legs – retaliated, launching a new wave of murders which claimed the lives of at least 18 men. In June 1982 a paramilitary group called Comando Condor issued a statement that it intended to 'finish off' homosexuals. One member of the Commission later appointed to investigate disappearances – *Comision Nacional Sobre la Desaparicion de Personas* (CONADEP) – estimates that at least 400 lesbian and gay men had been 'disappeared' though no mention of this is made in the Commission's official report, *Nunca Mas*.[7]

### Fundamentalist furies
In recent years some of the most violent examples of state-promoted homophobia have appeared in countries where fundamentalist religion and patriarchy are strong.

The coming to power in 1979 of Ayatollah Khomeini in Iran was swiftly followed by the execution of hundreds of gay people in Tehran. According to the Iranian gay-rights organization Homan around 4,000 lesbians and gays have been killed in the country since the fundamentalist Revolution.[10]

Public hangings – such as those of four young men in 2005 and another in 2006 – occur to a lesser extend these days. Often executions take place in secret, in prison, or even within families as 'honour killings'.

Recently the Iranian authorities have added extra charges – such as kidnapping, pedophilia or rape – to accusations of same-sex offenses in an attempt to dilute international criticism. 'It has hoodwinked even some human rights groups,' says Simon Forbes, who conducted a nine-month investigation based on information gathered from sources within Iran for the London-based group OutRage![11]

Homosexuality is also punishable by death in Saudi Arabia, though flogging is more common. In 2000, Amnesty International reported the execution of six men accused of committing homosexual acts; a further three were executed in 2002. However, there is at the same time a wealthy, male, gay scene of sorts centering on parties in private houses.

Journalist Brian Whitaker quotes one gay Saudi Arabian who comments: 'It's well known that there are several members of the royal family who are gay. No-one's chopping their heads off'.[12]

In Iraq homophobia has increased dramatically since the US-British invasion. Between 2003 and 2006 the local gay organization Iraqi LBGT recorded 26 homophobic killings of its members. In 2006 there was a surge of homophobic killings by state security forces and religious militias, following an anti-gay fatwa issued by the country's most prominent religious leader, the Grand Ayatollah Ali al Sistani. In May 2006 Iraqi police killed a 14-year-old boy, Ahmed Khalil, who had been forced into prostitution, and an 11-year-old called Ameer. Two young women, thought to be lesbians, were murdered in Najaf. Police tactics, developed in Iran, to entrap lesbian and gay people have been used in Iraq too. In 2007 a UN Assistance Mission in Iraq confirmed that there was an organized campaign to kill gays in Iraq.

Ali Hili is a gay activist who has been living in exile in London since 2006. As UK co-ordinator for Iraqi LBGT, he attempts to maintain contact with lesbian and gay compatriots who are trapped inside Iraq.

'They are at daily risk of execution by Shia death squads and the Sadr and Badr organizations,' he says. 'Members of these militias have infiltrated the Iraqi police and are abusing their police authority to pursue a plan to eliminate all homosexuals in Iraq.

'This is happening with the collusion of key ministers in the Iraqi government.

'What is happening today in Iraq is one of the most organized and systematic sexual cleansings in the history of the world.'[13]

Calls to violence have been made in the West too. In Australia in 2002 Sheik Shadi, an Islamic cleric, called for an Islamic court to be set up in that country, which would give Muslims the power to stone gay men and lesbians to death.

Meanwhile the popular English-language website IslamOnline has featured spokesperson Yusuf al–Qarasawi describing homosexuality as 'the most heinous crime', a sin so 'enormous in intensity and gravity' it must be punished in this world and the next. He urges that such 'deviants' be kept away from children.[12]

### Kill and cure

The West's most vociferous homophobia, however, is the Christian fundamentalist variety. Using the mass media – radio, television, internet – Christian fundamentalist preachers have taken their views to the airwaves with a vengeance.

The murder of young gay student Matthew Shepard by two young men in Wyoming was celebrated by a Kansas minister who used his website to praise God

---

**'Kill your son, your brother'**

Hussein, 32, is a gay man living with his married brother's family in Baghdad.

'I've been living in a state of fear for the last year since Ayatollah Sistani issued that fatwa, in which he even encouraged families to kill their sons and brothers if they do not change their gay behavior,' he says. 'My brother, who has been under pressure and threats from Sistani's followers about me, has threatened to harm me himself, or even kill me, if I show any signs of gayness.' ■

'Hunting Gays in Iraq – how the death squads work', Doug Ireland, October 2006, http://direland.typepad.com

---

for the murder.

Topeka, a Baptist organization in Kansas, holds anti-gay demonstrations near the funerals of people who have died of AIDS carrying placards asserting 'Gays Deserve to Die'. Another group calling itself STRAIGHT (Society to Remove All Immoral Gross Homosexual Trash) has dedicated itself to the cause of a 'fag-free America'.

There have been a number of homophobic murders and bombings of lesbian or gay meeting places in the US in recent years, perhaps encouraged by this kind of propaganda.[1] Amnesty International reports numerous attacks – physical and sexual – on lesbians and gays in US prisons, often under the incitement or with the complicity of guards.[14]

Not all are baying for blood however; there are more subtle approaches. Some organizations even present themselves as trying to 'help' gay people. The so-called Ex-Gay movement is dedicated to converting homosexuals to heterosexuality – using therapy, prayer or both. US organizations such as Exodus or the National Association for Research and Therapy of Homosexuality (NARTH) are well-funded and have centers would-be converts can attend, with teams of trained psychotherapists to hand. 'At-risk adolescents and parents,' says the NARTH website, 'have the right to know that homosexuality is preventable and treatable and the sooner intervention takes place, the better the prognosis.'

The effect of such therapies on young lesbian and gay people can cause great pyschological harm, warns the American Psychology Association.

Dr Rob Killian knows at first hand the despair that reparative therapy can provoke: 'Reparative therapy does not offer wholeness. It seeks to compartmentalize the unwanted feeling into a hated part of one's being that is buried and ignored.'[15]

If homophobia is fear and hatred of homosexuality

then reparative therapy, dressed up in caring piety, is an especially insidious and manipulative form of it.

## African panic

As we have seen, throughout the history of homophobia homosexuality has been described as 'someone else's' disease or sin or crime or custom or problem. Such thinking is nowhere more current than on the continent of Africa today. The emergence of clearly African gay organizations, inspired largely by the example of South Africa, has, paradoxically, led to a rash of homophobic pronouncements from political leaders and others.

President Yoweri Museveni of Uganda has been relentless in his insistence that gays and lesbians should be arrested, convicted, driven out of the country. His pronouncements have resulted in surges of homophobic violence in the country. The media also has its part to play.

'Nab him before he pollutes the population', urged a headline in the tabloid *Red Pepper* in September 2006, as part of its campaign to expose and punish lesbian and gay people in Uganda.[16]

Namibian leader Sam Nujoma holds that 'homosexuality must be condemned and rejected in our society'; he has ordered police to arrest, imprison and deport gays and lesbians. While Home Affairs

---

### Fanny Ann Eddy – Sierra Leonean pioneer

'When I went to open a bank account for the organization, the whole staff of the bank came out to have a look at me and I had to call the manager to make sure that I was actually served,' Fanny Ann Eddy told a gathering of 22 LGBT groups from 17 African countries.

A few months later, in October 2004, the tireless and fearless founder of her country's first LGBT group was dead – raped and murdered in the offices of Sierra Leone Lesbian and Gay Association she had founded two years earlier.

One of her suspected assailants was captured but later 'escaped' police custody. ■

## I was beaten beyond recognition

'Violence against gays is popular in Lagos. When they hear that someone is LGBT they will come round and beat you up... Two months ago a team of policemen came to my apartment and took me away to an unknown place for two days. I was beaten beyond recognition, and I am still receiving treatment for a head wound I received. I was dehumanized and paraded naked to the press. My money, ID card and shoes were taken.' ■

Chuma, 'Voices from Nigeria', IGLHRC, November 2006.

Minister Jerry Ekando called for their 'elimination'.[1]

Inspired by movements in South Africa and Zimbabwe, lesbians and gays have organized to fight prejudice in several sub-Saharan countries. But it is a risky business.

Anti-gay sentiment is especially strong in Nigeria, compounded by a Government campaign for new anti-gay laws. As in many sub-Saharan African countries, hatred is fueled to a large extent by Christian religion (see Chapter 6).

Faced with intense social rejection, many lesbian and gay people keep their sexuality tightly under wraps.

'I am a lesbian,' says Patricia, 'but because our society does not accept gays and lesbians I am in hiding. My family does not know. Only three of my friends know about it. My family would be extremely upset if they found out. They see it as a taboo. To them if I should be a lesbian something is wrong with me. I am out of my mind. I am a civil servant and I am afraid that if I came out at work, I would be fired.'[17]

### Why does homophobia happen?

The history of homophobia reveals an extraordinary array of ills laid at the door of people who depart from the heterosexual norm. They have been seen as sinful, pestilent, criminal, unnatural, sick, degenerate and unpatriotic. They have brought plague, poison, and threatened the family, state, natural order and survival of the human race. The anti-gay backlash caused by the AIDS epidemic was part of a long tradition.

Prejudices of all kinds abound in human society. But few have been quite so comprehensive in their range. In *The Anatomy of Prejudices* Elisabeth Young-Bruehl looks at such 'primary prejudices' as sexism, racism, anti-semitism and homophobia. She argues that they fall into one or another combination of categories: obsessional, hysterical, or narcissistic.[18]

Obsessional prejudice, by her definition, sees its objects as omnipresent conspirators or enemies set on one's destruction, who therefore must be eliminated. Hysterical prejudice interprets the hated individuals as 'other, as inferior, and as sexually threatening'. Racism is the best example of hysterical prejudice. Those who suffer from narcissistic prejudice 'cannot tolerate the idea that there exist people who are not like them'. She argues that homophobia alone fits all these categories, and this might help account for its persistence and prevalence.

Other psychological theories abound. The folk wisdom is that the most homophobic people are those who are repressing their own latent homosexuality. Certainly there is anecdotal evidence to support this. Homophobia does tend to occur most strongly in tight-knit macho units of men where homoeroticism is very much in the air but homosexuality is strictly forbidden. These men need to deny any sexual component to their bonding and can increase their solidarity by turning violently on 'fags' or 'queers' who are defined as completely alien. This is a phenomenon found amongst teenage gangs, police and soldiers. By attacking a gay person the individual attempts to make a clear distinction between himself (or herself) and the dreaded sexuality.

## Trendy hatred
Anti-gay sentiments may also be fashionable. In some places the term 'gay' has become a playground insult.

Popular culture may feed into this: the lyrics of some hip hop artists, the US's Eminem included, are redolent with homophobia.

Jamaican rap artists Elephant Man, Bounty Killer, Beenie Man and Buju Banton have written exceptionally violent lyrics that urge the shooting, burning, rape, stoning and drowning of gay people.

Gay people in Jamaica point to a close connection between the exhortations of pop musicians and homophobic violence. The island has one of the highest levels of popular violence against sexual minority people in the world and anti-gay assaults have taken the form of mob violence.

Two of Jamaica's most prominent gay activists, Brian Williamson and Steve Harvey, have been murdered. A Human Rights Watch researcher witnessed a joyous crowd gathered outside Williamson's house to celebrate his murder in 2004. Some sang 'Boom bye bye,' a line from a song about killing and burning gay men that was made a hit by reggae singer Buju Banton.[19]

Lesbians are not spared. In one song Elephant Man sings that it's 'not our fault' when lesbians get raped because 'two "sodomites" (lesbians) in bed are two women who should be dead'. In 2007 two young women, Candice Williams and Phoebie Myrie,

**Forms of persecution regularly practiced against sexual minorities around the world today:**
- unfair arrest
- unfair and unsubstantiated charges, especially of having sex with a minor
- beatings, torture and rape
- persecution at work, loss of employment
- bullying in schools and elsewhere
- invasion of privacy
- imprisonment, fines, flogging
- execution

believed to be having a lesbian relationship, were found murdered, their bodies thrown into a pit outside their home.[20]

## Youth in peril
Reasons given for harassing lesbian or gay people may be quite disarming in their simplicity. A gang of gay-bashing youths in San Francisco explained that they loved the thrill of the attack and of doing it together. They felt they could get away with bashing gay people in a way that they would not if they attacked say, women or people of color. Beating up 'fags' would not result in social disapproval, they felt. Some of those interviewed said they did not have anything particularly against gays – they were just easy targets.[21]

For young people school remains the place where most homophobic violence takes place.

This is what happened to US youth David Henkle:

'I was in the middle of the parking lot of my school and a group of [boys] surrounded me. They said: "let's string up the fag and tie him to the back of the truck and drag him down the highway"... They took a lasso and started throwing it around my neck... All I can remember is being surrounded by these people and how scared I was...'

This was the culmination of routine bullying for the 16-year-old. Distressed and hysterical he found the school vice-principal and told her what was happening. She laughed and told him to 'be more discreet' about his homosexuality.

No attempt was made to confront the bullies. David finally dropped out of school, aged 16, without finishing his studies.

This story is all too common. What is unusual is that David took his Nevada school to court for allowing persistent homophobic bullying and in 2002 won a landmark victory and compensation of $400,000.[15]

Pupils who do not fit gender stereotypes – such as

the 'Sissy-boy' or the 'Tom-girl' – are the most typical victims of bullying.

A Swedish lesbian reports being physically bullied every day for four years 'because they found me too butch'.[24] While Serkan Altan reports from Turkey: 'Any boy, aged eight or older who displays any hint of effeminacy, is very likely to be raped. Then the torture begins, especially in school. We homosexuals learn in school, along with other things, that we are going to be raped, beaten and tortured by the public and police.'[15]

In theory the UN Convention of the Rights of the Child provides strong protection against all forms of discrimination and violence. In practice the convention has rarely been invoked or used to the benefit of young LGBT people.

Bullying, bonding and scapegoating are all recognizable scenarios for how prejudice is acted out. But they only partly explain the mobilization of prejudice against sexual diversity. We need also to consider the politics of sexual control – the subject of the next chapter.

**1** *Homophobia*, Byrne Fone, Metropolitan, 2000. **2** *Hidden from History*, Martin Bauml Duberman, Martha Vicinus, George Chauncey eds, Penguin, 1991. **3** *Different Rainbows*, Peter Drucker ed, Gay Men's Press, 2000. **4** *Third Sex, Third Gender*, Gilbert Herdt ed, essay by Serena Nanda,

## Homophobia – roots and shoots

Zone Books 1993. **5** Cassell's *Encyclopedia of Queer Myth, Symbol and Spirit*, Randy P Conner et al eds, Cassell, 1997. **6** *The Men with the Pink Triangle*, Heinz Heger, Gay Men's Press, 1972. **7** *The Global Emergence of Gay and Lesbian Politics*, Barry D Adam, Jan Willem Duyvendak, Andre Krouel eds, Temple University Press, 1999. **8** 'Sexual Politics', Jeffrey Weeks, *New Internationalist*, November 1989. **9** *Amazon to Zami*, Monika Reinfelder ed, Cassell, 1996. **10** Homan www.homanla.org **11** 'Iran: The State-Sponsored Torture and Murder of Lesbians and Gay Men', Simon Forbes, Outrage!, April 2006. **12** *Unspeakable Love*, Brian Whitaker, Saqi, 2006 **13** Ali Hili of Iraqi LGBT speaking at Faith, Homophobia and Human Rights conference, organized by the LGCM, 17 February 2007. **14** *Crimes of Hate, Conspiracy of Silence*, Amnesty International, 2001. **15** *Sex, Love and Homophobia*, Vanessa Baird, Amnesty International, 2004. **16** www.mask.org,za **17** *Voices from Nigeria*, International Gay and Lesbian Human Rights Commission Report, IGLHRC, November 2006. **18** *The Anatomy of Prejudices*, Elisabeth Young-Bruehl, Harvard University Press, 1996. **19** OUTfront!, Lesbian, Gay, Bisexual and Transgender Human Rights. www. Amnestyusa.org **20** *Jamaica Star*, March 2007. **21** *Assault on Gay America*, Karen Franklin, 2000 www.pbs.org **22** Gay, Lesbian and Straight Education Network, 2005 www.glsen.org **23** Monograph Series No. 50 and published by the Australian Research Centre in Sex, Health and Society (ARCSHS), Faculty of Health Sciences, La Trobe University. **24** 'Social exclusion of young lesbian, gay, bisexual and transgender (LGBT) people in Europe' Judit Tacaks, ILGA/IGLYO, 2006

# 5 The politics of sexual control

**Strange bedfellows... family values... growing up gay... the best orgasms... authoritarianism... gender agendas... political pluralism... new parties, new diversities.**

FEW WOULD DESCRIBE Iran and America as natural allies. But those observing a debate at the United Nations in early 2006 might have been forgiven for gaining that impression.

When Iran blocked a resolution to grant sexual minority groups consultative status at the United Nations, its most vocal supporter was... the US.

All too often sworn political enemies have sung in sweet harmony when it comes to the issue of homosexuality. At times they even compete in their homophobia, each raising their voice louder than the other in protest and disgust.

This has been the case in Egypt, where the ailing secular government of Hosni Mubarak has been searching for ways to fight the rising popularity of its main opponent, the radical Islamist party of the Muslim Brotherhood.

Rather than appeal to the culture of sexual diversity that Egypt has traditionally enjoyed, Mubarak's government has launched a brutal campaign against sexual minorities.

## The Queen Boat

It started in May 2001, when police raided a floating nightclub called the Queen Boat in Cairo. Fifty-five men were arrested and while in police custody, some of them were suspended by the wrists, beaten with sticks and subjected to other forms of torture.

There followed a trial that received unprecedented publicity and was held in a court specially created for dealing with terrorists.

## The politics of sexual control

The accused were charged with 'the use of perverted sexual practices as part of their rituals; contempt and despite of heavenly religions and fomenting strife.'

The front page headline of a Cairo newspaper screamed: 'Perverts declare war on Egypt'[1]

Eventually, 21 were convicted of 'obscene behavior between men' – homosexuality is not illegal in Egypt – in a trial described by Human Rights Watch as 'an extravaganza rather than a judicial process'.

The Queen Boat case was the beginning of a crackdown on gay people, in which hundreds have been arrested, tortured and harassed.

### Family order

Why do they do it? Why do states get so exercised about sexuality? Is it just scapegoat politics or is there some deeper reason?

There is no single, simple answer. The psycho-social explanation is that social cohesion depends upon a certain degree of 'sexual repression' (in the language of Freud) or 'restraint' (in the language of the Moral Right). In this view certain forms of sexual behavior viewed as anti-social must be rejected for the social order to survive. This is the argument of those who would proscribe homosexuality because they see it as threatening their definition of 'the family'.[2]

The ideology of 'the family' has long been a rallying point for anti-gay organizations. Such groups claim that the institution of the family is breaking down due to the decline in sexual mores. Most of societal ills are laid at the door of this collapse of social cohesion. If sexuality is not controlled, then things begin to unravel. Homosexuality, for them, symbolizes a loss of control, of sense of purpose and of responsibility.

Founder of the Family Research Institute in the US Paul Cameron puts it this way: 'If all you want is the most satisfying orgasm you can get,' then homosexuality becomes 'too powerful to resist'. Marital sex, he says, 'tends toward the boring end'.

Anthony Falzarano of the Family Research Council sees homosexuality as a destructive force.[3]

'Basically the homosexual... is out to destroy traditional marriage, heterosexual marriage.'

The message coming from these organizations is that homosexuality is dangerous; it threatens to damage what is most dear to you – your family, your children, your grandchildren.

This may seem strange to sexual minority people who have families of their own, of one sort or another. These families may not follow the conventional model – but then nor do many heterosexual families, who increasingly do not conform to the nuclear mold. Families today come in all shapes and sizes, and a growing number of children have parents who are predominantly gay.

It could also be argued that homosexuality actually strengthens the family by liberating some adults from child-bearing duties and so increasing the pool of adults available to look after children.

But perhaps the main issue here is not so much 'the family' but power – and who gets to keep it. Feminists have shown how the ideology of the family, with its strict gender divisions, is the building block of patriarchy; socialist feminists have added that it is also the building block of capitalism.

The political uses 'the family' has served are quite apparent. In 1950s' North America and Europe the

---

### Different families

'I have two mothers and other kids don't. I feel different. I don't tell most of my friends I have two mothers, but the ones that know think it's nice. I don't tell other kids at school about my two mothers because I think they would be jealous of me. Two mothers is better than one'. ∎

Six-year-old interviewed in *Valued Families*, by Lynne Harne and Rights of Women, The Women's Press, 1997.

post-war assertion of patriarchy turned economically-independent working women into housewives and suppressed lesbian and gay life that had been emerging before the war. The family was all important and the woman's role in it was to be mother, housewife and spouse and support to the male breadwinner.[4]

During the 1980s' nuclear-arms-race era, presided over by Ronald Reagan and Margaret Thatcher in the West, 'family values' were again much trumpeted and homophobia was conscripted as an ideological weapon. It was a time of moral panic and insecurity: the nuclear build-up assured mutual destruction and AIDS had made its appearance. The family was constructed as a safe haven of traditional values and national security. Homosexuality was a threat to that.

Current fears around terrorism compound this need for 'safe havens' – be they physical, emotional or ideological. Politicians all over the world use the rhetoric of the family to show that 'they care'; that they can be trusted to protect that haven of human bonds in an insecure and rapidly changing world.

## Unsafe haven

But for many sexual minority people the traditional heterosexual family and its values is a very hostile place indeed.

'I'm not sure you're gay,' Lebanese teenager Ali was told by his older brother, 'but if I find one day you are gay, you're dead. It's not good for our family, our name.'[1]

Families often try to force 'normality' upon their deviant members. This is what happened to one young Zimbabwean in her family home under her parents' orders: 'They locked me in a room and brought him everyday to rape me so I would fall pregnant and be forced to marry him. They did this to me until I was pregnant.'[5]

In traditional societies a family's fortune can sink or swim on its reputation. Heterosexual marriage is compulsory. Failure to conform to this brings shame on your family, as sexual minority people living in such communities are well aware.

Maya Sharma has collected the experiences of poor and working class lesbians in India. One young woman, Manju, who is being coerced into an arranged marriage says: 'It is the right thing to do. Women have to marry. My brother worries because of me. Besides, people will talk if daughters of marriageable age are not married off.' In her view, only by agreeing to marry a man will she be able to maintain contact with the woman she loves. Another married woman fantasizes that one of her children and one of her female lover's children will grow up and marry each other, thus securing the bond between the two families and the two women's continuing relationship.[6]

Unsurprisingly, the forcing of lesbian or gay people into heterosexual marriage often ends badly. However,

---

### 'They said I was a sick liar'

'When there is something on television about this topic,' says a Hungarian 16-year-old who is not 'out' to his family, 'they start immediately that it is disgusting, that they are all pedophiles... My mother says that if I happen to be gay she will disinherit me. In her view it is a disease, some sort of neurological problem that should be cured'.

Emotionally and economically dependent on adults, a child or adolescent will have few options if the important people in her or his life react with hostility to signs of budding homosexuality or transgender behavior. Formerly loving parents may suddenly withdraw their affections and become threatening and coercive: 'When my parents assumed I might be non-straight,' reports one young Croatian lesbian 'they said it wasn't normal and I was a sick liar living a double life. Even though I had always been a perfect daughter, they said they were deeply disappointed in me. Sorry I was born. They said they couldn't look at me or talk to me ever again if I was lesbian or bisexual – that I would not be their daughter anymore. Then I denied it all and moved on with my "double life" in favor of keeping peace in the family.'[7] ■

stories of lesbians eloping with each other are featuring with increasing regularity in the Indian media.

But whether traditionalists like it or not, actual, real families are changing.

'Thank God my family accept me as I am and love me just the same,' says a gay 19 year old from Malta.

While a young lesbian in the Netherlands reports: 'In my family it is accepted very well. My aunt on my mother's side is a lesbian and the brother of my father is bisexual. This helps a lot.'[7]

In countries where they have been won, gay legal and political rights have also validated the creation of these new, alternative families and given them some protection from being torn apart by heterosexism.

One of the main advantages of anti-discrimination legislation in Ecuador, says activist Irene Leon, is that now if someone tries to take children away from a woman because she is lesbian she can refer to her constitutional rights.[8]

## Gender control

Although the threat to 'the family' is one of the most common ideological expressions of homophobia, the real objection is probably more deep-seated: it has to do with gender.

Deviation from heterosexual norms is threatening because it seems to challenge the conventional rules governing a person's sex, their sexual preferences and the general female and male roles in society.

The assertion of homosexual identity clearly challenges the apparent naturalness of gender roles. That women might find full emotional and sexual fulfillment with each other is clearly a threat to many heterosexual men.

The position, held by some lesbian feminists, that lesbianism is the logical response to male oppression, appears to confirm the conservative fear that homosexuality undermines the traditional roles of the sexes.

And if men establish primary relationships with each other this too suggests that there are ways of organizing emotional and sexual lives other than those approved of by religion and state.

Extremist religious leaders and their followers target sexual minorities and women first, observes Anissa Helie of the Women Living Under Muslim Laws Network. 'The very same rhetoric,' she says, 'is used to justify repression against homosexuals, feminists or 'different' women – who all are systematically denounced as non-Muslim, non-indigenous. It is always through manipulation of religious, national or cultural identities that violence is legitimized.'[8]

One reason sexuality and gender conformity are the focus of so much attention by fundamentalist forces, is that autonomy – especially for women – is a threat to authoritarian and patriarchal control.

## Absolutism versus pluralism

Homosexuality in itself may not pose a real threat to any established social order or regime. After all, various ultra-conservative regimes have tolerated a sort of closeted homosexuality. And the increasing prominence of gay conservatives – especially in the US and Britain – shows that liberalism around sex can be made to dovetail with economic liberalism.

The real threat comes when sexual-minority activities become part of an alternative way of life in societies where alternatives are not generally tolerated.

'When people endorse the idea of sexual pluralism,' argues social historian Jeffrey Weeks, 'they are also implicitly endorsing social and political pluralism. When they affirm their lesbian or gay identities, when they assert their sense of belonging to social movements and communities organized around their sexual preferences they are making a political statement. Homosexuality then becomes more than an individual quirk or private choice. It becomes a challenge to absolute values of all types. Authoritarian regimes don't like that.[2]

Those 'authoritarian regimes' may be governments or they may be authoritarian tendencies within societies, families, communities, individuals. The issue of homosexuality may not have attracted much attention, may have been brushed under the carpet, until lesbian and gay people start organizing politically. But when they start trying to create social and legal space for themselves, demand rights and forge sexual minority identities and communities, this provokes a reaction.

The Moral Right that emerged in the US during the 1980s was in a part an answer to the success of gay movements in that country.

In other parts of the world, gay rights have been cast as an unwanted import from the West, a symbol of Western domination and globalization.

'The enemy is still trying to come back with sinister maneuvers and tricks called lesbians and homosexuality and globalization... They colonized us and now they claim human rights when we condemn and reject them,' in the words of Sam Nujoma, President of Namibia.[9]

By resisting homosexuality leaders can appear to be resisting neo-colonialism and economic globalization, when in reality they are not.

Often a campaign against sexual minorities has been launched to distract attention from a deteriorating economic situation – a strategy employed by Robert Mugabe in Zimbabwe, Mahathir Mohamed in Malaysia and Hosni Mubarrak in Egypt too.

Political resistance to homosexuality also comes from communities within the West who want to assert their identities in opposition to 'immoral' Western lifestyles and who have their own separate political agenda to pursue.

If that political agenda is one of uniformity around

one set of beliefs and ideas about how people should and should not behave, then any form of diversity can be a threat.

Increasingly such authoritarian tendencies are working together, across national and faith boundaries, to form anti-equality coalitions on the international stage.

## New parties, new diversity

But there are contrary influences too. The collapse of authoritarian regimes in various parts of the world during the 1980s created some political and cultural space for sexual diversity. The break-up of the USSR threw up several new democracies – many of which set about scrapping old Soviet laws such as those outlawing homosexuality. Though social prejudice remains strong, the accession to the European Union of several eastern European states has pressured them into some degree of compliance with equality and anti-discrimination rules. Lesbians and gays in these countries are organizing, speaking out, creating LGBT subcultures and communities.

Latin American countries have turned their back on the bloody era of right-wing military dictatorships and welcomed the emergence of new political parties.

---

### 'Gays could be our savior'

Poland has seen rising political homophobia on the part of the Government as well as ultra-right and Catholic fundamentalist groups. But resistance is strong. Far from being put off by violent attacks on gay pride marchers, the small gay rights movement is growing and transforming itself into a larger civil rights movement.

'The gays could be Poland's savior,' says one Warsaw journalist. While Warsaw Pride's chief organizer, Tomasz Baczkowski, expected non-gays to outnumber gays at the 2006 parade.

'Our demonstration,' he said, 'was never a carnival like it is in the West, but instead was highly political – a parade for democracy. ■

From 'Poland's Criminal Probe of Gays', Doug Ireland, 9 June 2006. www.gaycitynews.com

---

## The politics of sexual control

These new parties of the Left have been far more positive to gay rights than their forbears.

In Brazil, militant lesbian and gay activists have worked hard with the Workers' Party to campaign for equality on all fronts, with considerable success. Anti-discrimination legislation now exists in some states and dozens of municipalities. And in 2006 Brazil became the first country in the world to launch a national campaign against homophobia. A record-breaking 2.4 million attended the gay pride parade in São Paulo. The theme of the parade, which received government funding, was 'homophobia is a crime'.

In Argentina the first transgender group was established in 1991 and in 2006 finally gained official legal recognition as a result of a Supreme Court ruling.

Meanwhile in Mexico, the macho traditions of the political Left have been challenged by the Zapatista Army of National Liberation. Since the earliest days of their rebellion the Zapatistas have embraced lesbian and gay struggles, inviting sexual minority representatives to their meetings and festivals. In the words of Subcomandante Marcos:

'What do lesbians, homosexuals, transsexuals and bisexuals have to be ashamed of? Let those who persecute the different be ashamed!'

In 1997 Patria Jiménez, lesbian, feminist and Zapatista activist, became the first openly gay MP in Latin America.

Even the Cuban regime has grown more tolerant in the past decade. 'Just frame your argument in Marxist orthodoxy and you can get away with anything,' is how lesbian activist Lupia Castro puts it.[11]

In Britain the Labour Party, which took over from the Conservatives in 1997, departed from its traditional indifference and/or hostility to gay-rights issues and introduced various changes, including equalizing the age of consent and introducing civil partnership. Chris Smith, Britain's first out gay MP, was joined by several other lesbian and gay new parliamentarians. He went on to become the first MP to reveal that he was HIV-positive.

Green parties in several countries adopted equality and anti-discrimination polices from the outset. And around the world pro-diversity coalitions of all kinds now exist. Sometimes they have been with other minorities: in Canada with the Quebec separatists; in Spain with the Basques. Progressive labor organizations have also become allies: in Canada, the US and Britain unions have played an important part in initiating and gaining sexual orientation protection.[4]

As suggested by the glowing examples of Ecuador and South Africa, joining forces with other human-rights and pro-democracy groups is politically most effective, and can bring change in those movements too.

## Political center stage

The support of the rights of sexual minorities can be seen as a touchstone for a just society; a way of measuring a society's commitment to pluralism and democracy.

As lesbian, gay and transgender people have gained increasing legal and political rights and several Western democracies now have 'out' gay and transgender politicians, you might imagine that diverse sexuality would have become less of a heated issue.

The opposite happened. Rather, sexuality has become a frontline of contemporary politics. Issues like gay marriage and gay adoption have sparked major political rows in the US and Britain, for example.

In Russia parliamentarians have witnessed three attempts between 2002 and 2006 to get homosexuality recriminalized. Nigeria and Tanzania have tried to rush through new anti-gay laws to 'protect' heterosexual marriage.

'It seems that for many the struggles for the future

of society must be fought on a terrain of contemporary sexuality,' comments Jeffrey Weeks. 'As sexuality goes, so goes society. But equally as society goes, so goes sexuality'.

And a key feature in that struggle is the one we tackle in the next chapter – religion.

**1** *Unspeakable Love*, Brian Whitaker, Saqi, 2006. **2** 'Sexual Politics' by Jeffrey Weeks, New Internationalist, November 1989. **3** *Global Sex*, Robert Altman, Chicago University Press, 2001. **4** *The Global Emergence of Gay and Lesbian Politics*, Barry D Adam et al, eds, Temple University Press, 1999. **5** *Amazon to Zami*, ed Monika Reinfelder, Cassell, 1996. **6** *Loving Women*, Maya Sharma, Yoda Press, 2006. **7** 'Social exclusion of young lesbian, gay, bisexual and transgender (LGBT) people in Europe' Judit Tacaks, ILGA/IGLYO, 2006 **8** New Internationalist, October 2000. **9** The Namibian 23 April 2001, www.mask.org.za **10** La Jornada,EZLN, 17 Hjune 1999. **11** *Different Rainbows*, Peter Drucker ed, Gay Men's Press, 2000. **12** *Sexuality – second edition*, Jeffrey Weeks, Routledge, 2003

# 6 Religion: gods and sods

**Nuzzling deer... laughing bonzes... sacred andro-gynes... Sodom revisited... fundamentalist vomit... ordination and schism... sex and the eco-system... new alliances.**

'I DON'T HAVE to feel no shame; in God's image I am made,' sang Boy George on his 'coming out' album *Cheapness and Beauty* – gently, ironically reclaiming religion from those who have conscripted it to oppress sexual minorities.

There has been nothing gentle or ironic about the hysteria surrounding homosexuality and religion in recent times. 'God hates fags' screams the slogan of Rev Fred Phelps' fundamentalist Baptist organization, Topeka, in the US. Homosexuals, says leading Shia cleric Ayatollah Sistani, 'should be killed in the worst, most severe way of killing'.[12]

Religious faith, often presented as 'culture', is increasingly invoked as a reason for discriminating against those who are not heterosexual or who bend gender rules in some way.

But what do the world's five main religions – Buddhism, Hinduism, Islam, Judaism and Christianity – actually have to say about same-sex desire or transgender?

## Buddhism

Buddhism appears the most positive towards sexual and gender diversity, though attitudes have varied according to culture and historical epoch.

The *Jataka* tales of early Buddhism, which originated in India, are generally favorable towards same-sex intimacy in their celebration of the Buddha's loving relationship with his disciple Anand. In one tale the two are depicted as deer always together, cuddling, muzzle to muzzle. In another, they are two young men who refuse to marry so that they may remain together.

However, between the third and fifth centuries AD same-sex intimacy and transgender behavior were being condemned by Indian Buddhists. Greatest hostility was directed towards 'third gender' or trans-gendered homosexual males called *pandakas*. These were forbidden to become monks. If discovered already living in a monastery, they were expelled. Other homosexual monks might also be expelled. Indian Buddhist nuns who engaged in lesbianism were punished but do not appear to have been expelled.

Chinese Buddhism showed greater tolerance – a view supported by tales concerning lesbian and trans-gender behavior among Chinese Buddhist nuns. A Buddhist nun founded the Ten Sisters Society, which embraced resistance to heterosexual marriage, pas-sionate friendship and lesbian intimacy, and held ceremonies of same-sex unions. This society became the prototype for other later societies including the Golden Orchid Association (see Chapter 3).

In Japan, homosexuality became even more closely aligned to Buddhism. In the early part of the Heian period (794-1185) Buddhist monks returning from Tang China in 806 are reputed to have 'introduced' homosexual practice – though, of course, it probably existed before then. By the end of the Heian period homosexuality had become popular among the aris-tocracy, perhaps because of the increased contact with the Buddhist clergy.

Expression of affection and desire by Buddhist priests for those they loved appears to have grown stronger over the following four centuries. In the mid-16th century, when Father Francis Xavier arrived in Japan with the hope of converting its people to Christianity, he was shocked to encounter so many Buddhist monks involved in same-sex relationships. He began referring to homoeroticism as the 'Japanese vice'.

Father Xavier decided it was his duty to rid Japan of 'the sin of sodomy'. He wrote: 'We frequently tell the *bonzes* [Buddhist monks] that they should not commit such shameful sins; and everything we tell them amuses them since they laugh about it and have no shame when they are reproached about so vile a sin.' It appears Xavier did not have much success. One report recounts how he and his missionaries were stoned by a gang of youths while walking through the streets of Yamaquchi, the youths yelling: 'So you're the ones who forbid sodomy!'

Of the four traditions of Tibetan Buddhism the Gelug (or Yellow Hat) has been associated with homoeroticism. The rule against heterosexual relations for monks seems to have encouraged same-sex relations. Numerous scholars, including Heinrich Harrar and E Schafer, have reported that same-sex relationships were very common in the Gelug monasteries of Tibet.

The impact of Buddhism on sexual minority people in the West has been considerable in recent years. A number of Buddhist lesbian and gay groups have been founded, including the Buddhist HIV/AIDS SODS project in Los Angeles. Author Gavin Harrison combines scenes from the Life of Buddha with his own gay identity and HIV-positive status to illuminate discussion of Buddhist principles.[1]

## Hinduism

Modern Hinduism appears quite hostile to homosexuality. Hindu fundamentalists from Shiv Sena and other groups hold the view that homosexuality is a Western import which is un-Hindu, un-Indian and has no place within the history, religion or traditions of the subcontinent.

However, research undertaken by scholars including Sadashiv Ambadas Dange, Alain Danielou and Gita Thadani has explored the issues of homosexuality and transgender within the tradition of Hinduism and other religions of the subcontinent.

Thadani's research on the pre-Hindu Indus Valley civilization of India shows how Goddess worship and acceptance of sexual variance was displaced by the far more patriarchal Hinduism. Yet many of the former elements remained, such as reverence of goddesses, deities of sensuality like Kama, Krishna, and Vasanta, and androgynous or transgendered deities like Ardhanarishvara. Ardhanarishvara is often referred to as a hermaphrodite, a primordial sacred androgyne.

According to Danielou, human homosexuals, hermaphrodites and transvestites can be considered sacred beings – 'images' of Ardhanarishvara.[1] Writer Mina Kumar has examined orthodox post-Vedic-Sanskrit literature in relation to homosexuality. She found that these texts regard lesbianism as illegal, immoral and diseased.

Some texts conflate impotency, homosexuality, transvesticism and being a eunuch in the word kliba, marking male homosexuality as trangressive because it is not procreative.

However she found that 'the cultural stream that draws more directly on popular traditions has generated more positive images of lesbians.'

The Tantric tradition, for example, values women's sexuality and provides 'a religiously sanctioned role for lesbianism'. The female organ is seen as the sole seat of all happiness. A sculpture in Bhubaneshwar depicts a woman kneeling, her face at the mons veneris of a standing woman whose right hand is raised in a pose that signifies her divinity.[2]

Transgender *hijras* (or eunuchs) consider themselves to belong to a separate, Hindu-related religious sect devoted to the Mother Goddess Bahuchara Mata. Arjuna, one of the heroes of the epic poem, the *Mahabharata*, is claimed by contemporary *hijras* (eunuchs) as one of their mythic forebears. A fierce warrior, Arjuna spends a year dressed as a member of the 'third sex' living in a harem, teaching women the arts of song and dance. Arjuna says: 'O Lord of the Earth, I will declare myself as one of the neuter sex. O monarch, it is indeed difficult to hide the marks of the bow-string on my arms. I will, however, cover both my arms with bangles. Wearing brilliant rings on my ears and conch-bangles on my wrists and causing a braid to hang down from my head, I will, O king, appear as one of the third sex. Vrihannala by name.'

A number of sexual minority groups currently exist on the Indian subcontinent – some using names that relate to traditional Indian concepts and culture.

## Islam

Muslim hostility towards same-sex eroticism is rooted in the tale of Sodom. Homoeroticism in general and anal intercourse in particular are referred to as *liwat*, while those (primarily men) engaging in these behaviors are referred to as *qaum Lut* or *Luti* or 'the people of Lot'. The prophet Muhammad is believed to have said: 'Doomed by God is [he] who does what Lot's people did... No man should look at the private parts of another man, and no woman should look at the private parts of another woman.'[1]

'The Qur'an [Koran] clearly states that homosexuality is unjust, unnatural, transgression, ignorant, criminal and corrupt,' declares the Jamaat-e-Islami, an extreme right politico-religious party in Pakistan.

But this is not accepted by all Muslims. Anissa Helie argues: 'In fact, the Qur'an is far from clear on the issue and the controversy regarding the position of Islam and homosexuality is ongoing. For some people, homosexuality is 'unlawful' in Islam; for others, the Qur'an does not clearly condemn homosexual acts.

The only actual reference to homosexuality in the Qur'an can be found in the sections about Sodom and

Gomorrah. While the harsh punishment inflicted on the people of Sodom and Gomorrah at the time of the prophet Lut [Lot] is for some people a clear proof that Allah meant to eradicate homosexual practice, others argue that there is no punishment specifically for homosexuality. The people of Sodom were punished for 'doing everything excessively'. They insist that it is not the Qur'an itself that brings condemnation of homosexuals but rather the homophobic culture prevailing in Muslim societies.[3]

Pre-Islamic traditions of the Middle East included goddess reverence, especially of the goddesses Al-Lat, Al-Uzza and Manat. These traditions were led primarily by priestesses and transgender homosexual males. With the triumph of Islam the earlier spiritual traditions were suppressed and their followers converted or were slain. The spiritual – and general – authority of women diminished greatly, and those engaging in same-sex eroticism and transgender behavior became outlaws. Aspects of this tradition survived, however, in Sufism, the mystical tradition of Islam.

The Sufis have for centuries suffered at the hands of other practitioners of Islam, due in part to their mystical focus and in part to their apparent acceptance of some forms of transgendered and homoerotic behavior. One Islamic text refers to the Sufis as a 'community of sodomites'.[1]

In *Sexuality in Islam*, Abdelwahab Bouhdiba explains that the Sufis were also singled out by reactionary Islamic authorities because they dared to look upon the male beloved as a reflection of God. This belief in embodiment, called *hulul*, was considered the 'most heinous of Sufi heresies'. Various punishments were meted out by the authorities to persons engaging in transgendered or homoerotic behavior, including stoning and burning. According to 12th-century scholar Ibn' Abbas, 'the sodomite should be thrown upside down from the highest building in the town, then stoned'.[5] Some Islamic faithful believed that in the afterlife 'punishment for sodomy will be even more terrible. On Resurrection Day, unless they repent, the guilty partners will find themselves stuck together'.

Since the 1970s the situation has become extremely difficult for gay and transgendered people living in countries dominated by certain radical forms of Islam (see Chapter 4). Fundamentalists also use religion against HIV-positive people. In 1997, Turkish Islamic physicians Mustafa Sener and Ibrhaim Geyik described AIDS as a divine warning to those who engage in corrupt lifestyles and they condemned other physicians for providing condoms 'instead of taking precise action against immoral and perverse sexual intercourse.'

However, some Islamic commentators have begun to reconsider the religion's – and the culture's – positions on same-sex eroticism and transgenderism. An editorial in *Islamic Canada Reflections* argues that while it 'is true that Islam forbids homosexual practice... this does not mean that gay people should be subjected to violent crime and other forms of persecution'.[1]

And an increasing number of gay Muslims are taking the risk of coming out of the closet and speaking out. The 2006 Euro-Pride parade in London had a strong and lively contingent aboard a green float, waving banners proclaiming: 'Muslim and gay.'

The Qu'ran is being re-examined by feminist and gay, or gay-friendly, theologians and believers in order to break the monopoly of male homophobic interpretation.

Writers like Shaid Dossani argue that Islam should be viewed as a vibrant faith which did not cease to evolve upon the death of the prophet Muhammad, and that while insistence on heterosexual relationships may once have served an important social function, it may now be time to embrace stable same-sex relation-

---

**The love I give my partner is very Islamic too**

Adnan Ali, founder of the UK branch of the gay Muslim organization Al Fatiha is used to receiving threats and abuse as a result of his mission to support isolated, scared and sometimes suicidal LGBT Muslims.

'The fact we exist is the greatest support for most people', he says. 'When I was growing up in Pakistan, I thought I was the only one on earth. I feel very proud to be gay and Muslim but it has taken me years. I thought at first I was Muslim so I could not be gay. Then I thought I was gay so I could not be a Muslim.

'All my first affairs of course were with people who were gay and Muslim, but no-one ever reconciled the two things. Interestingly, I met most of them at the mosques in Lahore. No, honestly – you could go just to cruise and meet people because they were such social places.

'[Today] I go to the mosque as a human being who wants to thank my creator – not as a gay or straight man. But Islam places a great stress on love and care and I think the love and care I give to my partner is very Islamic too.' ■

From: 'An Islamic revolutionary,' interviewed by Tania Branigan, *The Guardian*, 30 August, 2001.

---

ships as well.[3]

Syrian-born activist Omar Nahas tries to talk to imams (religious leaders) about homosexuality within Muslim communities in the Netherlands where he lives and works for the YOESUF foundation, an organization that provides information about Islam and male and female homosexuality.

'Homosexuality is a sensitive subject among Muslims,' says Nahas. 'Only with a great deal of patience, respect and careful choice of words can you get people to talk about it. You will have to create basic circumstances so that people tolerate your debates on creating tolerance towards homosexual people. These basic circumstances are best created from inside the religion itself.'[4]

For another Muslim writer, Khalid Duran, the way ahead for religious gays in Islam is to embrace Sufism, and put *tariqa*, the way of self-knowledge, in place of shari'a, customary Islamic law.[1]

## Judaism

The Old Testament puts it quite plainly: 'You shall not lie with a male as with a woman; it is an abomination. If a man lies with a male as with a woman, both of them have committed an abomination; they shall be put to death, their blood is upon them.'

'A woman shall not wear anything that pertains of man, nor shall a man put on a woman's garment; for whoever does these things is an abomination to the Lord your God' (*Oxford Annotated Bible*).

These passages from the Biblical books of Leviticus (18:22, 20:13) and Deuteronomy (22:5) have for centuries influenced the perspectives of Jews concerning same-sex eroticism and transgender. Biblical scholars suggest that the harshness of these commandments may be rooted in the efforts of the ancient Israelites to distinguish themselves from the Canaanites who had inhabited the land prior to their arrival. In Canaanite religion, both gender and sexual variance were associated with goddess reverence; in order to eradicate the religion of the Canaanites it was deemed necessary to eradicate erotic practices linked to that faith.

Despite the severe commandments of Leviticus and Deuteronomy, attitudes may have relaxed as struggles with the Canaanites lessened. Passionate friendship between members of the same sex were tolerated and even celebrated. Evidence of this shift may be found in the Biblical tales of David and Jonathan and of Ruth and Naomi. In later antiquity, however, hostility appears to have increased, exemplified by the writings of Philo Judaeas, living around 50 AD, who specifically linked homosexuality to the destruction of Sodom.

In the second-century rabbinical text – the *Mishna* – sexual intercourse between men becomes punishable by stoning. This continued into the Middle Ages. Several beliefs gained strength: men engaged in same-sex eroticism would be visited by divine punishment in the form of early death; earthquakes and solar eclipses were also seen as punishments for the sin of sodomy. The belief that homosexuality was associated with magic and idolatry resurfaced. In the late 12th century one of the first Jewish records specifically condemning lesbianism appears, in the writings of Moses Maimonides: 'Women are forbidden to engage in lesbian practices with one another, these being the doing of the land of Egypt.'

However, both esoteric and folk traditions of Judaism emerging in the Middle Ages seem to have treated gender and sexual variance less viciously. For example, the Jewish mystic Qabbalists explained androgyny as an attempt to restore the original androgyny of Adam, while folklore explained that the allegedly transgendered hare was the result of a mishap on Noah's ark and that this animal was blessed by the Lord.

This greater tolerance was mirrored by the dramatic rise of male homoerotic poetry among the Jewish poets of Spain. Often the beloved is compared to God – these are erotic spiritual poems as opposed to purely secular ones. Among Jewish poets who wrote poems of homoerotic love between the 10th and the 12th centuries the most famous are Moses Ibn Ezra, Yishaq ben Mar-Saul, Yosef Ibn Saddiq, Samuel Ibn Nagrillah, Solomon Ibn Gabirol, Judah-ha-Levi, Abraham Ibn Ezra and Isaac Ibn Ezra. These homoerotic poets were typically also lovers and spouses of women and would be considered bisexual in today's terms. With the expulsion of the Jews – who along with the Muslims, were accused by Spanish Catholics of bringing homosexuality to Spain – in 1492, this enlightened era appears to have ended. For the next four centuries little was written concerning gender and sexual variance in Jewish life.

Since the 1970s many gay-centred groups have been founded, including the World Congress of Gay and

Lesbian Jewish Organizations. Others, including the Central Conference of American Rabbis (Reformed) and the Reconstructionist Rabbinical Association, have adopted resolutions to support same-sex inclined Jews.[1]

Rabbi Arthur Waskow argues that religious precepts of the Torah – such as 'be fruitful and multiply' – reflected the needs of the time. Today, in light of the need to address climate change and the negative impacts of human development on the planet, he asks: 'Should we be encouraging, not forbidding, sexuality that avoids biological multiplication?'[5]

## Christianity

A few years ago a text was produced with the title *What Jesus Said About Homosexuality*. It contained blank pages. Prepared to comment on a whole range of moral issues and vices, Jesus of Nazareth had, it seems, nothing to say about homosexuality.

It is perhaps a little surprising then that the history of Christianity should be so replete with examples of persecution and condemnation of sexual minorities. Today most orthodox branches of the faith still actively discriminate against lesbians and gays on the basis that homosexuality contravenes 'Christian values'.

Where Jesus was silent, the Apostle Paul was not and his words have been widely used to condemn homosexuality. Referring to pagans, who rejected the one and only God, Paul states: 'God gave them up unto vile affections; for even their women did change the natural use into that which is against nature. And likewise also the men, leaving the natural use of the woman, burned in their lust one toward another; men with men working that which is unseemly, and receiving in themselves that recompense of their error which was meet' (Romans 1:26-28).[1]

The influential Christian theologian St Thomas Aquinas subsumed four categories of vice against

nature under the rubric of 'lust': masturbation, besti-
ality, coitus in an unnatural position, and 'copulation
with an undue sex, male with male and female with
female'.

Through the centuries, Christians – both lay and
cleric – have, of course, practiced homosexuality.
Thousands were executed, imprisoned or had to do
years of painful penance (see Chapter 4).

For lesbian, gay and bisexual individuals brought
up in the Christian tradition the best option was to try
and hide their sexuality and/or to distance themselves
from the religion.

But in the early 20th century the notion of an
explicit homosexual-centered Christianity began to
emerge. Elisar von Kupffer (also known as Elisarion)
founded the Klaristiche Movement which sought to
weave together homoeroticism, Greek religion and
mythology, and the medieval European code of chiv-
alry with Christianity.[1]

Derrick Sherwin Bailey's groundbreaking 1955
book *Homosexuality and the Western Tradition*
caused Christian writers and religious leaders to re-
examine the Bible to determine if anti-homoerotic
(and occasionally also anti-transgender) sentiments
were as intrinsic to Christianity as they had seemed.
Other important studies of this type followed. Many
of these, including Bishop John Selby Spong's *Living
in Sin* (1989) take issue with the interpretation of the
story of Sodom. The story, he argues, is chiefly concerned not with homosexuality but with the violation
of principles of hospitality.

Since the 1960s the idea that homosexuality and
Christianity can go together positively has been developed. An early pioneer was Michael Itkin, a priest in
the Eucharistic Catholic Church in the US, who developed a gay-centered theology, emphasizing links with
pacifism and civil rights. Also in the US, Reverend

## Sodom revisited

According to Bishop Spong, the men of Sodom who ('to a man') gather around Lot's house demanding he send his two guests out to them so as they may 'know them' are probably seeking to humiliate the two strangers. It is extremely unlikely that all the men of Sodom are homosexuals. When the 'good man' Lot offers to send out his virgin daughters to the mob instead, are we to assume that offering girls up for gang rape is what fathers are supposed to do? And when Lot, after the city had been destroyed by God, impregnates his two daughters are we to assume that incest is to be commended too?

Spong says: 'Perhaps the more important issue is one of gang rape which seems to be the intention of the men of Sodom. Is gang rape ever right, regardless of whether it is homosexual or heterosexual in nature? Lot seems to think that homosexual gang rape was evil, especially since it violated the Middle Eastern law of hospitality, while the heterosexual gang rape of his daughters would be acceptable since no hospitality laws were at stake. Is it right to assume that the condemnation of homosexual gang rape is to be equated with the condemnation of homosexuality per se? I think not, and further believe that anyone who reads this Biblical narrative with an open mind will discover that the real sin of Sodom was the unwillingness on the part of the men of the city to observe the laws of hospitality.'[6] ∎

Troy Perry founded the gay-centered Protestant Metropolitan Community Church in 1968. 'The Lord is my shepherd and he knows I'm gay,' Perry insisted. Other groups followed. One of the most original contributions of this period was Catholic priest Richard Wood's *Another Kind of Love: Homosexuality and Spirituality* (1978) in which he defined a 'gay spirituality'. Lesbian Episcopalian priest Carter Hayward, meanwhile, has linked the 'making' of love with the 'making' of justice. Opposing all this has been the orthodox Catholic Church and the growing, mainly Protestant, Fundamentalist Christian Movement. Among the best known leaders in the US are Jerry Falwell, Pat Robertson and Jay Grimstead (famous for his slogan 'Homosexuality makes God vomit').

The orthodox Catholic Church and right-wing

## Religion: gods and sods

Catholic organizations such as Opus Dei have also adopted an increasingly aggressive stance.

Pope Benedict has maintained a position that homosexuality is an 'intrinsic moral evil' and 'an objective disorder' and declared gay marriages as 'false'. In 2003, while he was still Cardinal Ratzinger, he asserted that 'allowing children to be adopted by persons living in such unions would actually mean doing violence to such children'.[7]

This prompted many to draw attention to the violence done to children by the Catholic Church which has a long and shameful history of protecting pedophile clergy at the expense of child victims of sex abuse.

### Unholy row

Within the international Anglican Congregation homosexuality has become a subject of deep division and acrimony. Although closet gay clergy are by no means uncommon, ordaining would-be priests who are open and honest about their homosexual orientation is another matter. South Africa's former Anglican Archbishop, Desmond Tutu, is a strong spokesperson for equality and the ordination of lesbian or gay priests. He sees 'the persecution of people because of their sexual orientation' as 'every bit as unjust a crime against humanity as apartheid'. He adds: 'All over the world, lesbian and gay people, bisexual and transgender people are persecuted... We treat them like pariahs... We make them doubt that they too are children of God – and this must be nearly the ultimate blasphemy...'[8]

His fellow African, the archbishop of Nigeria Peter Akinola, takes the opposite view. He sees acceptance of homosexuality as 'yielding to the permissive and satanic spirit.' He sees the call for equality as an 'attack on the Church' which will pollute and weaken it. 'Homosexuality does violence to nature', he argues.

And he goes further: 'This lifestyle is a terrible violation of the harmony of the eco-system... As we are concerned about the depletion of the ozone layer, so we should be concerned by the practice of homosexuality.'[9]

The battle has become fierce. Crisis point was reached in August 2003 when the openly gay Rev Gene Robinson was appointed bishop of New Hampshire in the US. Outraged traditionalists, both in the global North and South, threatened schism.

For several years now the once hushed topic has prompted stormy exchanges at annual meetings of the Synod as the Anglican Church continues to wrestle – some say tear itself apart – over the issue of lesbian and gay priests. Transsexual priests, it seems, are easier to accept.

Other Christian churches have been more open. Protestant Unitarians teach that homophobia – not homosexuality – is the sin. The United Church of Canada, one of the country's largest Christian bodies, has an explicit policy of accepting and ordaining gay and lesbian clergy. Quaker congregations accept and conduct blessings of gay long-term relationships on exactly the same basis as heterosexuals.

### Human-rights issue
Throughout human history, religion has often been used to oppress one or another group of people. Dogmatic inconsistencies together with the ebb and flow of acceptance and rejection, tolerance and intolerance, are indicators that religious prejudice against sexual minorities is rarely intrinsically religious at all. Most often it is political at root and has to do with asserting or maintaining power or superiority. Religiously-inspired prejudice has often been whipped up to control believers and marginalize those who do not strictly conform or who might challenge the central authority of the keepers of the faith. It is also used as a tool of xenophobia.

## Religion: gods and sods

In the post 9/11 world, 'interfaith dialogue' has become a popular buzzword. It is seen as a means to counter the threat of violent religious extremism epitomized by Al Qaeda.

But interfaith dialogue may be compounding the problem facing women and sexual minorities. Increasingly traditionalists of different creeds are joining forces to resist women's rights (to abortion, for example) and LGBT rights. Internet preacher Sheikh Ahmad Kutty says that 'working with non-Muslims to make the streets free from homosexuality is a religious duty'.[10] While in Moscow, Christian, Jewish and Muslim clerics joined forces to try and prevent the city's gay pride parade from going ahead in 2006.

But other alliances are possible. A conference on Faith, Homophobia and Human Rights held in London in February 2007 brought together several hundred LGBT people from an array of different beliefs and positions – Christians, Muslims, Hindus, Jews, Buddhists, Humanists. They were able to reach a remarkable degree of consensus.

The way ahead, as articulated by Clara Connolly of the Women Against Fundamentalism network, may be 'an alliance of people of all faiths and none' to combat religiously inspired homophobia.[11]

**1** Cassell's *Encyclopedia of Queer Myth, Symbol and Spirit*, ed Randy P Conner, David Hatfield Sparks, Mariya Sparks, Cassell, 1997. **2** *Facing the Mirror: Lesbian writing from India*, Ashwini Sukthankar, Penguin, 1999. **3** New Internationalist, October 2000. **4** New Internationalist, October 2000. **5** World Congress of Gay, Lesbian, Bisexual and Transgender Jews. www.glbtnews.org **6** 'Sodom revisited', Bishop John Selby Spong, New Internationalist, November 1989. **7** *The Boston Globe*, Michael Paulson, 7 June 2005. **8** *Sex, Love and Homophobia*, Vanessa Baird, Amnesty International, 2004. **9** 'Why I object to Homosexuality and Same-sex Unions', Peter Akinola, http://www.anglican-nig.org **10** *Unspeakable Love*, Brian Whitaker, Saqi, 2006. **11** At 'Faith, Homophobia and Human Rights' conference organized by the LGCM, London, February 2007. **12** www.petertatchell.net

# 7 Science: explaining sexual orientation

Questing the source... from ferrets and fruitflies... gay sheep... hormones and chromosomes... 'cures' for homosexuality... the 'gay brain'... the 'gay gene'... to... who cares?

THE SEARCH FOR the scientific 'source' of homosexuality has led down many varied – and some decidedly strange – paths.

For a long time it was assumed that same-sex behavior was a strictly human phenomenon. Deemed 'unnatural' it was thought not to exist in the animal world. Often naturalists and biologists just weren't looking out for it – or did not recognize it when they saw it.

More recent studies have found evidence of homosexual behavior in a wide range of species of birds and mammals. A few of the more entertaining observations are that:

- Male orang-utans enjoy fellatio.
- Male walruses sodomize each other.
- In summer months, killer whales devote a tenth of their time to homosexual activity.[1]

In 2007 the Natural History Museum in Oslo mounted an exhibition entitled 'Against Nature?' It featured some of the 1,500 species in which homosexuality has been observed, ranging from insects to sperm-whales.

Studies of sexual desire in animals suggest behaviors and preferences that are similar to human sexual orientation. The discovery of 'gay' fruitflies has featured large in recent attempts to try and prove a biological basis for sexual orientation.

What has been described as a 'significant incidence of lesbian seagulls' was seen off the coast of California in the 1970s. Attempts to find them again in 1996 failed, but the birds were committed to immortality by the song 'Lesbian Seagulls' from the movie *Beavis and Butthead Do America*.[2]

For several years researchers in Oregon conducted experiments on gay sheep – believed to constitute around a tenth of the sheep population. Early findings appeared to support the theory that same-sex behavior is biologically 'hard-wired'.

But in early 2007 the program sparked intense controversy when claims were made that the scientists were trying to 'turn gay sheep straight'. This was denied by the researchers but not before the row had prompted the headline 'Sheep have the right to be gay, says Martina Navratilova.'[3]

### Enter the doctors

Since ancient times philosophers, such as Plato, have pondered the mysteries of sexual desire and orientation. But from the late 1800s scientists, physicians and mental health specialists have pursued these lines of inquiry with increased vigor. Initially the special interest in homosexuality was connected to the desire to cure or eliminate what was seen as sexual perversion.

In Chapter 2 we saw how gay jurist Karl Ulrichs, influenced by contemporary embryology, developed his quasi-scientific 'Uranian' explanation of sexual orientation. Ulrichs sent his theories to psychiatrist Richard von Krafft Ebing in 1866. The latter took on board many of these ideas in his *Psychopathlogia Sexualis*, but he also significantly modified them. Ulrichs' view that homosexuality was natural and congenital was altered to fit a criminal/medical model which emphasized perversion, sickness and deficiency. Ulrichs was to come to see Kraft Ebbing and other 'doctors of the insane' like him not as allies but as his 'opponents'.[4]

The phrase 'sexual inversion' was to become the more common medical term and it was used by British sexologist Havelock Ellis in his study of that name in

1897. *Sexual Inversion* popularized the idea of 'inversion' as an inborn gender anomaly. The book's gay co-author, John Addington Symonds, felt strongly that homosexuals should be considered as a 'minority' group but gave way to Ellis' preference for viewing homosexuality as a neurosis and a congenital abnormality in the hope, proven vain, that this would gain sympathy and tolerance from the public. Up to 1910 much of the degeneracy-theory/evolutionary-theory literature on homosexuality appears in medical journals or in books that were not readily accessible to the public. The more salacious parts were printed in Latin. The first English edition of Ellis' *Sexual Inversion* was suppressed and sales of the American edition were at first restricted to doctors and lawyers. Newspaper and magazine coverage was almost non-existent. *The Lancet*, Britain's leading medical journal, refused to review *Sexual Inversion* lest people read it.[4]

## Enter the psychologists

In the middle of the 20th century most popular were theories of sexual orientation that saw early sexual experiences as crucial. It went like this: if you had pleasurable sex with someone of a particular gender you would want to go on having sex with someone of that same gender in future. If the sex were unpleasurable, though, you would not. One indication of the continuing hold of these theories is the notion that a person, especially one who is sexually inexperienced, can be seduced or recruited into becoming lesbian or gay. This 'seduction theory' implicitly accepts that people will 'naturally' develop into heterosexuals unless seduced into homosexuality by a predatory homosexual.

Another cluster of theories – called 'family dynamics' – says it is all to do with one's relationship with one's parents. As usual, the study focused mainly on men. The classic version stems from Freud's Oedipal theory and sees male homosexuality as the result of

## Kinsey's 7-point scale

Possibly the most eye-opening and best popularized set of studies to emerge in the past 100 years were those of US researcher Alfred Kinsey and his colleagues in the mid-20th century.

In their extensive interviews researchers Kinsey, Pomeroy and Martin found a significant number of men and women with histories of both heterosexual and homosexual experiences and/or psychological responses.[2] From this they determined that 'the heterosexuality or homosexuality of many individuals is not an all-or-none proposition'. To deal with this they developed a 'classification based on the relative amounts of heterosexual and homosexual experience or desire in each individual's history. Known as the Kinsey 7-point scale, it rates as follows:

  **0** Exclusively heterosexual with no homosexual
  **1** Predominantly heterosexual, only incidental homosexual
  **2** Predominantly heterosexual, but more than incidental homosexual
  **3** Equally heterosexual and homosexual
  **4** Predominantly homosexual, but more than incidental heterosexual
  **5** Predominantly homosexual, only incidental heterosexual
  **6** Exclusively homosexual with no heterosexual
  **X** No social-sex contacts or reactions

Kinsey's insight was a departure from the binary view of sexual orientation and offered a bi-polar view which saw sexual orientation as continuous: each person's sexual orientation falls somewhere on the scale between two extreme poles. ■

having a strong mother and a distant father, while male heterosexuality is the result of having a strong identification with the father, relinquishing the mother and replacing her with other women. More recently psychologists have articulated versions of 'family dynamics' theories relating to women, some seeing lesbianism as a result of failure to identify with the mother or remoteness from her.

Some sociobiologists have even developed 'parental-manipulation theories' which suggest that parents unconsciously determine that it would be better for them if their family focused its reproductive and survival resources on the offspring of certain children but not others.

One of the most widely believed 'common-sense' theories of how sexual orientation develops focuses on the extent to which a child's behavior is gender-typical or atypical. Every known culture associates somewhat different behavioral stereotypes with men and women. A gender-typical child conforms to these and will go on to be a heterosexual. But sissy boys and tomboy girls are likely to become homosexual, the theory goes. According to some versions of this theory, something about the experience of engaging in gender atypical behaviors as children shapes a person's sexual desires as an adult.[2]

Many lesbian and gay people themselves feel that nothing 'made them gay'. To them their homosexuality is an essential, fixed characteristic and there is no matter of choice in it. Andrew Sullivan, former editor of the US *New Republic*, is a firm believer in this: 'For the overwhelming majority of [homosexual] adults the condition of homosexuality is as involuntary as heterosexuality is for heterosexuals and... is evident from the very beginning of the formation of a person's emotional identity.'

However the fact that many people may feel it to be so, does not necessarily make it so. As Edward Stein points out: 'People are not reliable at discovering the source of something so complex as their own sexual disposition simply through introspection.'

He draws the analogy of class. You might feel that you belong to a certain social or economic class and you have little choice in the matter. But that does not make your class an innate biological property. 'Sexual orientation,' he says, 'may be a certain social human kind, not a natural kind.'[2]

That would certainly be the view of social construction theorists. They hold that sexuality is socially constructed and lesbian, gay, bisexual and heterosexual identities are all historically contingent. They are categories formed in and by society with particular purposes. In the words of writer and academic Elizabeth Wilson: 'Sexual identity and sexual desire is not fixed and unchanging. We might create boundaries and identities for ourselves to contain what might otherwise threaten to engulf or dissolve into formlessness.'[5] Social or cultural construction theories were especially popular with the lesbian and gay liberation movement in the 1970s and 1980s. However, the notion of gay or lesbian identities was often viewed somewhat ambivalently, as a complex, contradictory but necessary tool of resistance against heterosexual patriarchy.

In more recent times, however, the social construction theories have been turned against gay communities by their enemies – the Moral Majority and their anti-gay organizations. They argue that if sexual identity is socially constructed then it can also be socially deconstructed. Hence the Ex-Gay Movement's belief that it can 'convert' homosexuals to heterosexuality.

Meanwhile, interest in finding biological causes for sexual orientation has boomed.

## The biologists' turn

The idea that perhaps the secret of sexual orientation lies within the body is less threatening now to gay people than it might have been in an earlier era. The fact that some of the researchers are themselves openly gay helps.

Looking to the body for an answer is not new, of course. In 1916 geneticist Richard Goldschmidt was suggesting that homosexuals might be people whose bodies did not match their sex chromosomes. This theory was accepted by various thinkers in the early part of the century, including sexologist Magnus Hirschfeld. It was disproved in the 1950s, however.

Other scientists focused on levels of hormones in the bloodstream, sex glands or urine. Experimenters claimed that lesbians had higher levels of testosterone and lower levels of estrogen than heterosexual women, and gay men had lower levels of testosterone and higher levels of estrogen that heterosexual men.

Even before 'sex hormones' (such as testosterone and estrogen) were isolated, some scientists believed there were differences between heterosexuals and homosexuals in the structure and/or the secretions of the sex glands. These hypotheses led to attempts to 'cure' lesbians and gay men through various surgical and hormonal treatments, including castration and in some cases testicle transplants.[6]

Attempts to 'cure' people of their homosexuality based on theories involving internal bodily differences continued in North America and Western Europe until the late 1970s, despite lack of any concrete evidence of success. In fact, most gay men treated with testosterone experienced an increase in their sex drive without any change in object of desire.[2]

## The gay brain

Others hold that the difference between homosexuals and heterosexuals is 'in the brain' and significant recent research has concentrated in this area.

In 1991, Simon Le Vay, a neuro-anatomist at the US Salk Institute, published a study of the size of particular cell groups in the hypothalamus – a small region of the brain, slightly smaller than a golf ball. The hypothalamus plays a key role in sex, diet, cardiovascular performance, control of body temperature, stress, emotional response, growth and other functions.

Le Vay's idea was to focus on areas of the hypothalamus that are thought to be different in men and women. Many scientists believe that at a certain point in fetal development the human brain exhibits difference according to sex: that men tend to have one sort of brain and women another. The extent to which this is so, however, is very small and quite controversial. Le Vay reasoned that, given that most people who are primarily attracted to women are men and vice versa,

## 'Cures' for homosexuality

**Since the late 19th century doctors have tried to develop 'cures' for homosexuality - without much success.**

**Prostitution therapy** Through sex with prostitutes, 'inverted men' would experience heterosexual desire.

**Marriage therapy** When presented with the option of courting and marriage, the 'deviant' would naturally go straight. Severe study of abstract (like math) would help.

**Cauterization** New York researcher Dr William Hammond suggested that homosexual patients be 'cauterized [at] the nape of the neck and the lower dorsal and lumbar regions' every 10 days.

**Castration or ovary removal** Removal of testes to eliminate sex drive in male homosexuals. If homosexuality is hereditary, removal of reproductive organs would provide long-term cure.

**Chastity** If homosexuality could not be cured, then homosexuals had no moral choice but to remain chaste.

**Hypnosis** US doctor John D Quackenbos claimed that 'unnatural passions for persons of the same sex' could be cured through hypnosis.

**Aversion therapy** Used during the first half of the 20th century, this rewarded heterosexual arousal and punished homosexual attraction, often through electric shock.

**Psychoanalysis** In the 1950s, Dr Edmund Berger spoke of homosexuality as a kind of 'psychic masochism' in which the unconscious sets a person on a course of self-destruction. Find the cause, such as resentment toward a domineering mother, and you find the cure.

**Radiation treatment** X-ray treatments were believed to reduce levels of promiscuous homosexual urges brought on by glandular hyperactivity.

**Hormone therapy** Steroid treatments to 'butch up' the boys and 'femme out' girls. Prolonged use could cause sterility and cancer.

**Lobotomy** By cutting nerve fibers in the front of the brain, homosexual drives (and most sexual and emotional reaction capabilities) were eliminated. Lobotomies for homosexuality were performed until the 1950s in the US.

**Psycho-religious therapy** Religious doctors and therapists combined religious teachings with psychoanalysis to inspire heterosexuality.

**Beauty therapy** All a butch lesbian needs is a good make-over by a beauty stylist (but not a male homosexual one). ■

Adapted from 'Thirteen Theories to "Cure" Homosexuality' by Don Romesburg, in *Out in All Directions: A Gay and Lesbian Almanac*, Lynn Witt et al, eds, Warner Books, 1995.

to discover where sexual orientation is reflected in the brain he should look in the parts that are structured differently in men and women.

He examined 41 brains: 19 from gay men who had died from AIDS; six from straight women, and 16 from men presumed heterosexual. He found that the part of the hypothalamus known as the 'INAH-3' was significantly smaller in gay men than in those presumed to be heterosexual and was about the same size as those of women. This seems to suggest that gay men's INAH-3 is, in a sense, 'feminized'. Le Vay claimed that the study opened the door to finding an answer to the question 'what makes people gay or straight'.

His theory has been challenged, however. The fact that all the male subjects with smaller INAH-3s had died of AIDS and that at the time of death virtually all had decreased testosterone levels as a side-effect of treatments, was seen as significant. Also, no brains of lesbians were examined, which if the theory were correct, should show larger INAH-3s.[2]

## The gay gene

The idea that sexuality might be hereditary has been around at least since medieval times. Recently, though, it has taken the form of the hunt for the so-called 'gay gene'.

A leading researcher in this field is biologist Dean Hamer of the US National Cancer Institute. Hamer began his study by looking at families of gay men. In the early 1990s he placed an ad in a Baltimore gay newspaper under the headline: 'Gay Men – Do You Have Gay Brother?'

Having isolated what he took to be a pattern of maternal-linked inheritance in the families of gay men, he did a genetic linkage study to determine where on the X-chromosome the gene responsible for this pattern is located.

Hamer's most significant result was that he

detected an increased rate of homosexuality on the maternal side of gay men's families. But commentators have expressed concern about this result and its significance. Some have said the different rate of homosexuality among maternal and paternal relatives is not statistically significant. Partly this is because Hamer's conclusions are founded on seeing a base rate of homosexuality within the general population at two per cent. If the base rate is actually four per cent or higher, as some argue it is, his results are not statistically significant.

In 1993 and 1995 Hamer pinpointed a specific genetic marker on the X-chromosome linked to homosexuality in men. He found that in 40 pairs of gay brothers, 33 had the same set of DNA sequences in a region of the chromosome called Xq28.

This study was immediately used by gay activists who were hoping that the discovery of a gay gene would strengthen their case against discrimination. But when Ontario neurologist George Rice tried to replicate those findings, he could not.[7] Rice himself didn't discount the idea of a genetic link to homosexuality – but he didn't think Xq28 was the spot. 'The search for genetic factors in homosexuality should continue,' he maintained.

Groups opposing gay rights latched onto Rice's result, claiming it confirmed what they had been saying all along: that there is no 'gay' gene, that homosexuality is a 'lifestyle' choice that deserves no legal protection.

### Who cares?

And so, the search – and the controversy – continues. In the US especially, the hunt for a biological link to homosexuality has become politically highly charged.

But does it really matter where sexual orientation comes from? Do we need to pinpoint this? The chances are that sexual orientation has multiple origins. Some theories will work better for some people, some for others. Some of us may be able to plausibly argue a whole range of possible 'explanations'. Different pieces of personal history can be used to fit different theories. Ultimately – and most gay rights groups agree on this – the origins of sexuality should make no difference to civil, political and human rights. Equality does not require scientific justification.

Scientific investigation into sexual orientation is interesting, fascinating even, and provides a rich field of work for researchers. But what is the point of such research? For the average lesbian, gay or bisexual person, it may be of little relevance. Those who oppose gay rights have their agenda to pursue and if medical science cannot be used to support their cause then something else will be.

There might also be considerable risks attached to, for example, finding a 'gay gene' in a society where homophobia exists and full civil rights for sexual minorities do not. Could it lead to gene therapy to 'cure' gays? Prenatal tests to detect the gene in the womb – and subsequent abortion of gay fetuses? Or prenatal therapy to try and turn gay babies into heterosexual ones?

Medical science continues to be a double-edged sword for lesbian, gay and bisexual people. The same is also true for transgendered people, whom we come to next.

1 *The Penguin Atlas of Human Sexual Behavior*, Judith Mackay, Penguin, 2000. 2 *The Mismeasurement of Desire*, Edward Stein, Oxford University Press, 1999. 3 'The intriguing tale of gay sheep', Johann Hari, The Independent, 4 January 2007 4 *The Myth of the Modern Homosexual*, Rictor Norton, Cassell, 1997. 5 *The Cultural Construction of Sexuality*, Pat Caplan ed, Tavistock Publications, 1987. 6 *Queer Science: the Use and Abuse of Research into Homosexuality*, Simon Le Vay, MIT Press, 1996. 7 ABC News, 22 April, 1999.

# 8 Transgender and intersex: 'as the stars in the sky'

**There's more to gender than 'his' and 'hers'... genital mutilation Western style... 'third genders'... the eunuchs of India... human rights... and trans liberation.**

'IS IT A boy or a girl?' tends to be the first question asked when a baby is born. And a cursory look at the genitals usually provides the answer.

Meet a person for the first time and you will probably automatically, unconsciously, register whether that person is male or female. If you can't place them, you may find yourself searching for clues. For some reason, it seems important to know.

Most of us are culturally heavily conditioned to categorize sex and gender in this binary, dimorphic way. But actually life and nature are a lot more complex than that.

Until comparatively recently most public knowledge of transgender issues came from 'shock-horror' style newspaper articles. They might be revelations of women who had 'passed' most of their lives as men and vice-versa. Or, in less sensational mode, they might be autobiographical accounts by people who had had 'sex change' operations as gender reassignment was more commonly called. Usually those who told their stories were male-to-female transsexuals, who spoke of having felt, since an early age, that they were 'trapped in the wrong body'. British travel writer Jan Morris was one who famously described her experience of gender as something more 'spiritual' than biological, a feeling that has been echoed by many trans people.

Today more and more transgendered (or trans) people are 'coming out'. In so doing they have revealed the extent to which the human rights of transgendered individuals have been – and continue to be – violated.

But they have also become part of a growing – and increasingly successful – campaign for change.

The sheer variety of people 'coming out' and the research that has gone into the subject reveals a far more complex picture than previously imagined. The fact that many transgendered people, post-therapy or operation, are also gay or lesbian, is especially puzzling to the heterosexual mainstream.

A much richer, more diverse reality exists. It includes female-to-male (FTMs) and male-to-female (MTFs) transsexuals; transvestites or cross-dressers; intersexuals or hermaphrodites (born with ambiguous genitalia), eunuchs (in India, *hijras*). It includes people who are transgendered in the sense that they live their lives as a gender different from their biological sex but have done nothing to alter their biology; people who have had partial or total gender reassignment through surgery and hormone therapy; others who have elected for hormone therapy alone.

It includes people of various sexual orientations – gay, straight, bisexual – and people who switch between gender identities. And if that is not quite complex enough, some trans people describe themselves as 'male-to-male' or 'female-to-female' to reflect the feeling that they have always deep-down been the gender they feel themselves to be, regardless of social or biological assertions to the contrary. The possibilities and definitions seem infinite. Many people just settle for the simple, blanket term 'trans'.

Meanwhile, anthropological studies reveal transgender expressing itself in ways that are culturally quite distinct, with frames of reference that are not always translatable. Transgender in Peru is not the same as in Indonesia; being trans in North America may bear little resemblance to the experience in Namibia. What is certain, however, is that transgender is widespread and in its emergence from the closet is challenging fixed ideas about gender more radically

> ## 'Why create categories?'
>
> *Vimlesh, a factory worker in Rajasthan is talking to researcher Maya Sharma:*
>
> **Vimlesh:** In the factory no one mocks me to my face. I am not bothered by others' opinions. Everyone has a right to eat what they want, wear what they want, live as they choose. From the beginning I have dressed this way, like a man. And I have always preferred women. Why is it so, I have never thought about that too deeply. But it is not important to have an answer to everything. Why create categories, such a deep difference between male and female? Only our bodies make it different. We are all human beings aren't we?
>
> **Maya:** Bodies make us men and women.
>
> **Vimlesh:** Is that so? Tell me something, do bodies alone make us men and women? First of all, we are not that different when we are young... When my body began to change like all men and women's bodies do, I felt strange. I did not like it. Besides, no one had prepared me for these changes. I did not know about these things. But I had to accept the law of nature. I thought, because of these changes I cannot stop living. I had to overcome the shock, adjust to these new developments in my body. But I hate the life of a girl. If I could I would ask Brahma why he made me a female in body. If it was within my control, I would change my body just as I have chosen to wear men's clothes. But I say I am a man. I choose to be one. ∎
>
> From *Loving Women – Being Lesbian in Unprivileged India*, by Maya Sharma, Yoda Press, 2006.

than ever before. And it's happening everywhere, from metropolitan New York to small town India.

## Enigmas and variations

Chi-Chi lives in a village in the Dominican Republic where a rare form of 'pseudo-hermaphroditism' was recorded among numerous families in the early 1970s.

Chi-Chi's mother had 10 children. Three were girls, three boys 'and four are of this special sort', she says. 'I knew that this sort of thing existed before I had my own kids. But I never thought that it would happen to me... I told them to accept their destiny, because God knows what he's doing. And I said that real men often achieve less than those who were born as girls. And that's how it turned out. My sons who are real men haven't achieved as much as the others.'[1]

The medical explanation is that, while still in the womb, some male babies are unable to produce the testosterone which helps external male genitals to develop. They are born with a labia-like scrotum, a clitoris-like penis and undescended testes.

Chi Chi is at ease with the situation. 'Whatever I feel, that's the way I am. I was born as a girl, and that girl died one day and a boy was born. And the boy was born from that girl in me. I am proud of who I am. A lot of people actually envy us,' Chi Chi tells filmmaker Rolando Sanchez in the documentary *Guevote*.

The film portrays the daily lives of Chi-Chi and Bonny, two 'pseudo-hermaphrodites', and the way in which their families, partners and other villagers respond to them.[2]

For some scientists the phenomenon – which locals call *guevedoche* or 'balls at twelve' – presented an ideal 'natural experiment' that would help them to prove once and for all that hormones are far more important than culture in the development of gender identity. A research team headed by Julliane Imperato-McGinley proposed that in a laissez-faire environment, with no medical or social intervention, the child would naturally develop a male gender identity at puberty, in spite of having been reared as female.[3]

Not everyone agreed with this simplistic approach. Ethnographer Gilbert Herdt pointed out the guevedoche were different and they knew it as they had compared their genitals with those of girls during public bathing. Villagers, who were familiar with the guevedoche over generations, accepted them as a 'third sex' category, sometimes referring to them as machi-embra (male-female).[4]

But not all wanted to adopt a male gender identity after puberty. In *Guevote* Bonny relates the case of guevedoche Lorenza: 'She had more chances as a woman. Lots of men fell in love with her. She always wore women's clothes and had very long hair. That's why she wanted to stay a woman and not become a man.'

Here then is a community that recognizes the actual existence of 'third sex' people as part of human nature and creates corresponding gender roles to accommodate them. It's an attitude that enables Bonny to say: 'If I am like this, God will know why... If I feel good, why should I change things? This is how I grew up, why look for something else?'

## The law and the knife

Such an accepting approach to gender ambiguity has not been the pattern in most of the Western world. Far from it: binary is the rule. We are, in the words of trans activist Leslie Feinberg, faced with 'two narrow doorways – female and male'. But some people just don't fit those doorways. When faced with official forms to fill in they cannot tick either the 'M' box or the 'F' one. They do not officially exist, unless they fit the binary model – or are made to fit it.

Since the routine practice of correcting the ambiguous genitalia of intersex children began in the US and Europe in the late 1950s, debates have raged about whether gender identity and roles are biologically determined or culturally determined.

The work of John Money and colleagues at Johns Hopkins University and Hospital, Maryland, has had a major impact on the treatment of intersex children, transsexuals and other sex-variant people.

Money advised on the famous case of the identical twin boy who had been reassigned as a girl after he lost his penis in a circumcision accident at the age of seven months in 1963. The child underwent plastic surgery to make his genitals female-appearing and he was treated with female hormones at adolescence.

Between 1973 and 1975 Money reported a completely

favorable outcome and this became the key ca[se] [in the] following 20 years. The case influenced the tr[eatment] of boys born with 'too small' penises, and led to the recommendation that their penises and testes be removed and the boys be surgically reassigned as girls before the age of three 'to grow up as complete a female as possible'. In these cases quality of life was based on ideas of adequate heterosexual penetration. According to the Johns Hopkins team, the twin had subsequently been 'lost to follow-up'.

But this was not so. As it turned out, the twin did not feel or act like a girl and had discarded prescribed estrogen pills at age 12. She had refused additional surgery to deepen the vagina that surgeons had constructed for her at 17 months, despite repeated attempts to convince her she would never find a partner unless she had surgery and lived as female. At the age of 14 the twin refused to return to Johns Hopkins and convinced local physicians to provide a mastectomy, phalloplasty and male hormones. He now lives as an adult man.[5]

## Banishing ambiguity

Intersexuals, popularly referred to as 'hermaphrodites', are usually born with genitals somewhere between male and female – rarely with two complete sets as in myth. The number of such births is more common than most people realize, with the highest estimates in the US at four per cent of births. That's some ten million children, annually.[6]

According to the Intersex Society of North America one in every 2,000 infants is born with ambiguous genitalia from about two-dozen causes. There are more than 2,000 surgeries performed in the US each year aimed at surgically assigning a sex to these intersex patients. The Intersex Society campaigns against what it sees as the unethical medical practice of performing cosmetic surgery on infants who cannot

---

**FACTS**

• One in every 12,000 people is a male-to-female transsexual.[1]

• One in every 30,000 is a female-to-male transsexual.[1]

• One in every 1,000 people has a body that does not categorize them as male or female.[2]

• One in 1,666 people has chromosomes that are not 'normal' XX (female) or XY (male).[2]

Source: 1 *The Penguin Atlas of Human Sexual Behavior*, Judith Mackay, Penguin, 2000; 2 Intersex Society of North America www.isna.org

---

give consent. Founder of the Intersex Society, Cheryl Chase, believes that 'most people would be better off with no surgery'.

'Genital mutilation,' she points out, 'is a phrase that's easy for us to apply to somebody who belongs to a Third World culture, but any mutilating practice that's delivered by licensed medical practitioners in our world has an aura of scientific credibility.'[7]

As children many intersexuals have undergone repeated unexplained examinations, surgery, pain and infection. In most cases the children have been 'lost to follow-up'. Consequently, there has been no reliable medical data to assess the effects of surgery or to provide guidance for future practice.

Surgeons admit that they are attempting to alleviate a 'psycho-social emergency' rather than a medical one. But instead of helping intersex children and their families or friends to accept difference, doctors whip up a crisis which they can then fix with available medical technology. Ambiguous genitals are referred to as 'deformed' before surgery and 'corrected' after. But the reported experience of intersexuals who went through this in childhood is a sense of having been 'intact' before surgery and mutilated after it.

When she was 12 one woman was told that she needed surgery to remove her ovaries because she had cancer. What actually happened during the operation was her clitoris and newly-descended testes were removed.

The view that 'it is easier to dig a hole than build a pole' accounts for why most intersex individuals are made into girls. But surgery is also performed on baby girls as young as six weeks who have vaginas considered 'not deep enough', even though this is not always successful and has to be repeated at various stages as they grow up.[5]

In 1994 Chase and others began gathering stories into a newsletter called *Hermaphrodites with Attitude*. The first issue had a picture of Rudolph the Rednosed Reindeer on the cover, with a hand-colored red nose on each copy. The accompanying article satirized medical literature on intersex genital surgery by discussing Rudolph's nose as a disfiguring deformity, and an 'after surgery' picture captioned 'excellent cosmetic result', clearly depicted a mutilated Rudolph in tears.

Some medical experts have their doubts about 'corrective' surgery too. Dr George Reiner, Assistant Professor of child and adolescent psychiatry at Johns Hopkins University, warns against placing too great an emphasis on the genitals, pointing out that 'the brain is the most important sex organ in the body'.[8] Psychologist Suzanne Kessler concludes that genital ambiguity is 'corrected' because it threatens not the infant's life but the culture the infant is born into.

While trans activist Zachary Nataf asks: 'What about compassion and faith in the ability of the parents to cope with their own emotional pain and distress about their child's "imperfection" and to nurture that child despite their difference? What about the rights of the child, especially the right of the child to decide their gender identity, if different from what the experts have designated it to be?'

Colombia is one of the few countries to legislate in favor of the rights of the child in such cases.[9]

## Complex genders

Actually identifying a person's gender is far more

complex than most people imagine. There are no absolutes in nature, only statistical probabilities. We all begin life with a common anatomy which then differentiates if there is a Y chromosome present. This activates the production of testosterone, appropriate receptors in the brain and the formation of testes. The other features which do not develop remain in the body in vestigial form.

Several factors can be taken into account in determining a person's biological sex. They include chromosomal sex (X and Y, for example); hormonal sex (estrogen and testosterone); gonadal sex (ovaries and testes); genital sex (vagina and penis, for example); reproductive sex (sperm-carrying and inseminating; gestating and lactating); and other associated internal organs (such as the uterus or the prostate).

These factors are not always consistent with each other. In fact science admits everyone falls somewhere along a continuum. But few people would know if they were 100-per-cent male or 100-per-cent female, chromosomally or hormonally, as there are not many cases in everyday practice in which this would be tested. Unless you want to take part in the Olympic Games that is, in which case you would have to undergo a chromosome sex test, although this has been abandoned as unfair and unreliable by other sports

---

**The curious case of Iran**

In 1976, the supreme leader of Iran, Ayatullah Ruhollah Khomeini, issued a fatwa to allow people with hormonal disorders to change sex if they wished, as well as change their birth certificates. Recently 70 transsexuals were registered at the Khomenei Relief Center, a non-governmental organization that loans money to transsexuals to help them pay for surgery and to provide psychological assistance. Athena, 20, and Milad, 30, are two of many transsexuals in Iran. The pair, who met three years ago at the center, became good friends as a result of undergoing the same life experience. ■

From 'Women of the Axis', Caroline Mangez, Paris-Match, 25 August 2005.

---

bodies. The *British Journal of Sports Medicine* claims that one in 500 athletes would fail the chromosome sex test. This is because chromosome variations do not necessarily affect physical appearance. A test might determine an athlete is not a woman for the sake of competition, but that certainly does not make her a man in her everyday life. Other indicators of sex are subject to similar variations. Even the capacity to reproduce is not a clear indicator: some intersexuals have had children. The so-called biological line between male and female is frankly quite fuzzy.

British trans activist and academic Stephen Whittle writes: 'Currently medicine recognizes over 70 different intersex syndromes and one in every 200 children will be born with some sort of intersex matrix. For some this will never be discovered, whereas for others it will only be discovered when they attend a fertility treatment clinic later in life. Furthermore the work of the Netherlands Brain Bank on brain sex determination has indicated that transsexual people should possibly be included in the range of physical intersex syndromes as it supports the hypothesis that there is a brain sex difference between men and women; and transsexuals have the brain sex of that gender group to which they maintain they belong.'[10]

So much for sex. But sex is not gender. Sex is biological. Gender is social, cultural, psychological and historical. It is used to describe people and their roles in society, the jobs they do and the way they dress, how they are meant to behave.

A person's gender is usually assigned at birth. The 'boy' or 'girl' which is documented on the birth certificate affects almost everything else that happens to that child socially for the rest of his or her life.

### The third gender
Responses to gender ambiguity vary from culture to culture. The two-sex/two-gender model is by

no means universal. One of the most humane and enlightened approaches was observed in the 1930s among the Native American Navajo people. The Navajo recognized three physical categories: male, female and hermaphrodite or nadle. Nadles had a special status, specific tasks and clothing styles, and were often consulted for their wisdom and skills. Also known as *berdache* (see Chapter 3) these existed in other Native American groups. A person would become a berdache, would move into the third gender for spiritual and personal reasons. They did not change their bodies. They changed gender without changing sex – a change that was culturally acceptable, without concern for biology. No stigma was attached to them or their lovers or partners either.

In India the *hijras* have a 2,500-year-old history. Known contemporarily as a 'third gender' caste, hijra translates as hermaphrodite or eunuch or 'sacred erotic female-man'. Some are born intersexual, others are castrated. But the community also attracts a wide range of transvestites, homosexual prostitutes and religious devotees of the Mother Goddess Bahuchara Mata.[4]

Hijras are viewed as a third sex and there is a social place for them in Indian society. It's not, admittedly, an elevated place – they are perceived as somewhat discredited, associated with fallen women, prostitutes, marginals.

But they do have a subversive power. It is considered bad luck to turn hijra minstrels away from important events like weddings and not to pay them for their somewhat risqué song and dance routines. Hijras can bless children, and curse adults, to earn a living; their powers exercise symbolic control over life and death, notes anthropologist Serena Nanda in her authoritative study.[4]

They claim as their own caste all children who are anatomically hermaphrodite, or who have a strong desire to become hijras. In doing so they may provide a lifeline to young gender outcastes, abused and rejected by their families and communities.

Many contemporary hijras resort to prostitution as a means of survival. Some Indian men prefer sex with hijras as they will consent to sexual practices which women are reluctant to engage in. Interviews conducted by Serena Nanda indicate that those who chose to become hijras did so due to their homosexuality: 'We dress like girls because of the sexual desire for men.' Others earn a living as debt-collectors, and a few are even making a career for themselves in politics.

'You don't need genitals for politics. You need brains.' This unusual but true slogan came from Shabna Nehru, the first eunuch politician to run for Parliament in India.

She did not get in, but her record as a municipal councilor for Hisar is exemplary. She has outshone her peers at getting water, sewer lines and roads for

## Sachin's story

Sachin always felt like a girl and was treated like one, doing domestic duties around the house. At the age of 17 neighbors and relatives began to tease and harass Sachin. His elderly parents did not defend him. Instead they asked him to leave the village, to avoid the shame he was bringing upon them.

'That night I cried a lot. I realized that my parents' respect in society was much more important than their own son. I drank some poison, hoping to kill myself. But I started throwing up which woke my parents. They rushed me to hospital where I recovered. I told my parents: "You wanted me to leave but I have nowhere to go. No education. No skills."'

But Sachin left home and went to the town of Tirupathi. There an old man came up to him as he sat outside the temple crying.

'I told him my complete story. I told him I liked wearing saris, make-up, flowers in my hair. He heard my story and told me about the hijra community. He asked me to go and join them. That was the first I heard about hijras.' ∎

From *Human Rights Violations Against the Transgender Community*, Report by People's Union for Civil Liberties (PUCL-K), Karnataka, 2003.

her district. 'I used to entertain people by dancing,' says Shabna. 'Now I entertain them by doing good, humanitarian deeds.'

Some people suggest that, without children or family, eunuchs are the perfect antidote to India's political corruption and nepotism.

## Violence and vulnerability

In most parts of the world, however, powerful taboos against gender ambiguity still prevail, underpinning fear and discrimination. 'Sexually ambiguous bodies are threatening,' suggests trans activist Zachary Nataf. 'Perhaps they elicit desire, possessing it might seem an erotic potential beyond those with ordinary genitals. Maybe the notion of sex or gender mutability provokes a kind of terror or gender vertigo.'

These and other factors may render transgender and gender ambiguous people especially vulnerable to violence and to ridicule. They are discriminated against in employment, often not getting jobs, however well qualified. Many lose their jobs if they cross-dress or embark on reassignment therapy. A comparatively high number of male-to-female transsexuals go into prostitution – partly because of the difficulty in getting other employment, partly to raise cash for operations. This makes trans people more vulnerable to HIV infection and violence on the street.

According to Amnesty International, transgender people are often attacked in ways that strike at key manifestations of their identity. Those arrested by police may be stripped, beaten and forced to perform sexual acts. In numerous cases male-to-female trans people have been beaten on their cheekbones or breasts to burst their implants, sometimes causing the release of toxic substances with severe health consequences.[12]

Sometimes religious powers are invoked to try and exorcise the spirits that are thought to be causing gender confusion. This is what happened to Ugandan Victor Juliet Mukasa, who even as a little girl rebelled fiercely against the female gender identity – and clothing – that she felt was imposed upon her. Eventually she found herself standing in front of a 1,000-strong congregation in one of Uganda's popular Pentecostal church healing events. The pastor declared Victor was harbouring a male spirit from the Indian Ocean.

'The pastor started laying hands on me and all his boys in the healing ministry came and laid hands over me and started taking off my garments one by one. Some of them were trying to slap the spirit out of me, they were laying hands on my private parts to get the male spirit out. I was really fighting because I did not want them to do what they were doing. And they believed it was the demon trying to fight them. They threw my clothes on a fire they had made. I was stripped naked. I used to bind my breasts at the time. And when they touched this part of me it was so humiliating, I cried. And every time I cried they would call it liberation.'

Victor came to realize that religion was a large part of the problem facing trans people like herself. With two other women she set up Freedom and Roam Uganda, a lesbian, bisexual, transgender women's organization.[13]

Victor's experience was dramatic. But in many more hidden and mundane ways trans people are routinely badly treated. Using health services can be an ordeal – reports of humiliation and worse are common. As a result many avoid seeking medical help when sick. And in many countries trans people cannot get important documents altered to reflect their gender following reassignment – denying the possibility of marriage and causing humiliation, aggravation and arrest on suspicion of using false documents.

In recent years, however, trans campaigners have won important victories, especially on the legal front. Most countries in Europe now give transsexual people the right to change birth certificates (see Appendix). Many recognize the right of transsexuals to marry in their post-operative sex. Similar rights have been extended in Korea, Japan and Aotearoa/New Zealand which has a transgender parliamentarian. In Canada and the US there are some new trans-friendly laws, but they vary from state to state.

## The challenge

These legal advances are highly significant. But there are many diverse ways in which the Transgender Movement is challenging the tyranny of the two-gender model and the human-rights abuses that arise from it.

Take British artist Grayson Perry who collected his prestigious Turner Award in his favoured garb of billowing dress, wig and ankle socks, while accompanied by his wife and daughter.

And although many transsexuals still want to achieve a congruence of identity, role and anatomy by having sex-reassignment surgery, an increasing number are deciding against surgery, without compromising their core gender identity. It's simple. Some men don't have penises and have vaginas, some women have penises and don't have vaginas.

More and more transgendered people are choosing to be 'out', making it easier to build a social movement. Zachary Nataf explains: 'As a transgendered man (female-to-male transsexual) I do not "pass" as simply male but am "out" in order to campaign for non-discrimination and Transgender Pride. I did not choose to be transsexual, nor did I change gender roles in protest against society's oppressive gender system. I did it to achieve an authenticity and outward expression of a deeply abiding sense of myself as a gendered being. During transition I became more fully and truly myself, suspending the symbolic hold society's rules had over my body in order to achieve it. The rigidity of the rules is what is not natural.'

### 'As the stars in the sky'

Assertiveness is replacing shame and secrecy. Questions are being asked, answers demanded. 'Gender and genitals comprise the stronghold of control binding all people to a social order that has serious difficulty

---

**Alive, not trapped**

'I cannot say that I was a man trapped in a female body. I can only say that I was a male spirit alive in a female body, and I chose to bring a male spirit alive in a female body, and I chose to bring that body in line with my spirit, and to live the rest of my life as a man.' ■

Jamison Green, US fiction writer, essayist and public speaker.
From *Reclaiming Genders*, Kate More and Stephen Whittle eds, Cassell, 1999.

tolerating diversity or change,' says trans activist Jamison Green. 'Somebody's got us by the balls and they don't want to let go. Who is that somebody? Who is so afraid of losing control?'[10]

Scholars are opening out areas previously sealed off in academe. 'How many sexes and genders have there been?' queries Gilbert Herdt as he takes to task the paradigm of unquestioned two-sex/two-gender model that has stalked Western thinking, restricting even that of progressives like Darwin and Freud.

The two-sex system is not inevitable. It's just a product of societies hung up on reproduction, concludes Herdt. 'We need an anthropology and social history of desire that will lead us to closer approximations of understanding the lived realities of peoples themselves,' he says.[4]

As the space for them opens up, the reality is being made by trans people themselves. More transgender and intersex people are opting to live bi-gendered or hybrid gendered lives, choosing hermaphroditic bodies, through surgery, to match their core sense of who they are. Activist Michael Hernandez says: 'I have found a balance, a sense of peace. I am more than male and more than female. I am neither man nor woman, but the circle encompassing both... I just am. The name and the fit aren't that important any more... Gender and behavior are as variable as the stars in the sky. There is no typical pattern which provides definitive proof that one is transgendered.'[14]

Campaigner Leslie Feinberg comments: 'The women's liberation movement sparked a mass conversation about the systematic degradation, violence and discrimination that women faced in this society... This was a big step forward... Now another movement is sweeping onto the stage of history: Trans Liberation. We are again raising questions about the societal treatment of people based on their sex and gender expression. This discussion will make new contributions to human consciousness.'

The struggle has the potential to liberate all of us, whatever our gender or sex, from rigid, stereotypical ways of being masculine and feminine.

1 *Guevote*, Rolando Sanchez, Fama Film AG, Bern, Switzerland, 1997. 2 This chapter draws extensively from Zachary I Nataf's article 'Whatever I feel', *New Internationalist*, April 1998. 3 *New England Journal of Medicine*, Julliane Imperato-McGinley et al, 'Androgens and the Evolution of Male Gender Identity Among Male Psuedo-Hermaphrodites', No 300, 1979. 4 *Third Sex, Third Gender*, Gilbert Herdt ed, Zone Books, NY, 1994. 5 *Hermaphrodites with Attitude Quarterly*, Bo Laurent, Fall/Winter, 1995-96. 6 'Quelle Difference? Biology dooms the Defense of Marriage Act', David Berreby, High Concept (Website: www.surfablebooks.com/wbmedical/). 7 San Francisco Chronicle, David Tuller, 'Intersexuals begin to Speak Out on Infant Genital Operations', 21 June, 1997. 8 *Clinical Psychiatry News*, Katherine Maurer, vol 25, No 7, July 1997. 9 IGLHRC, 2000. 10 *Reclaiming Genders*, Kate More and Stephen Whittle eds, Cassell, 1999. 11 'Taboo Breakers', *New Internationalist*, October 2000. 12 *Crimes of Hate, Conspiracy of Silence*, Amnesty International, 2001. 13 *New Internationalist*, May 2007 14 *Trans Liberation*, Leslie Feinberg, Beacon Press, 1998.

# Conclusion: defending the rainbow

A YOUNG MAN gets up at the back of the hall and starts talking nervously. He tells the 200 or so people gathered in a building overlooking the River Thames, that his boyfriend has been murdered in this city. The killers are now out to get him, he says. For that reason he has gone into hiding.

The shocked silence is almost audible. The young man goes on. He wants to know what is going to be done to stop those who are preaching and promoting the homophobia that has killed his lover and now threatens him.

The man does not give his name. Nor does not disclose his nationality – that might identify him. He is an immigrant, a refugee – brave but frightened and vulnerable.

His intervention puts the proceedings into a different perspective. Up to now much of the discussion has been about securing rights – principally employment rights of one kind or another. This man is talking about the right to stay alive; not to be murdered just because he is gay. It's hard to know what to do or say. Expressions of sympathy and solidarity seem inadequate somehow.

But there are things that people living in countries where there is greater acceptance of sexual diversity can do. One is to lobby governments and join campaigns to stop the deportation of sexual minority people back to countries where they will be persecuted, either by states that criminalize homosexuality or by societies that punish it.

The other is to give solidarity and support to LGBTI groups and their members in countries where they are being targeted. This can be done through various human rights organizations (See Contacts and Action page).

As this book has detailed, the plight of LGBTI

people living in countries such as Jamaica or Nigeria or Iran is extreme. But there is still homophobia in more privileged corners of the world too. Many sexual minority people are living in families or communities or environments where their sexuality is reviled and where they have to keep it hidden. Some will be dealing with a complex of prejudices around race, religion, gender or class as well as sexuality.

And even for the comparatively privileged the struggle for sex rights is not over. While much has been achieved and translated into law, at a profound level very little has changed. Most societies remain largely defined by heterosexual attitudes and assumptions. Gender stereotyping remains resolutely strong, especially in the treatment of young children. In terms of attitude, progress on transgender is painfully slow.

It's hard to know what lies ahead. Perhaps the march towards sexual diversity will continue. Perhaps we will in time reach a point where sexual diversity – including heterosexuality – is accepted as the norm, homophobia as the aberration. That would appear to be the goal of the International Day Against Homophobia (IDAHO) campaign. At that point maybe sexual identities won't be necessary any more.

Or perhaps rows over sexuality and gender non-conformity will rage on, creating even deeper divisions between peoples, communities, societies and cultures. Perhaps LGBTI people will continue to be the scapegoats or pawns in conflicts over who gets to decide how people are to live.

There are certainly those who are using the issue of sexuality for their own ideological ends. Right-wing US-funded evangelical groups are loudly preaching an anti-gay message in the African countries in which they are gaining ground, the money they bring influencing local political agendas in ways that are damaging to both sexual minorities and to women.

## Conclusion: defending the rainbow

One thing that seems certain is that the fight for sex rights and for sexual diversity has a way to go. Whatever happens next is likely to have implications for all of us for it will help determine the kind of societies – and the kind of world – we live in.

### 10 Action Points

1 Repeal laws criminalizing homosexuality.
2 Condemn torture, whoever the victim.
3 Provide safeguards in custody: take measures to prevent rape of LGBTI people.
4 Prohibit forced medical 'treatment': this amounts to torture.
5 End impunity: investigate allegations of torture or ill-treatment of LGBTI people.
6 Protect LGBTI people against violence in the community: police and other authorities have a duty to make clear that homophobic violence will not be tolerated.
7 Protect refugees fleeing torture based on sexual identity: governments should review and amend asylum policies to eliminate bias.
8 Protect and support LGBTI human-rights defenders.
9 Strengthen international protection: numerous UN instruments could be used to prevent torture and ill-treatment, if ratified.
10 Combat discrimination: adopt constitutional and other provisions prohibiting all forms of discrimination based on sexual orientation or gender identity. ∎

# Action & Contacts

## INTERNATIONAL

### International Gay and Lesbian Human Rights Commission (IGLHRC)
www.iglhrc.org
Tel +1 212 268 8040
Campaigns for equality and documents abuse and discrimination worldwide.

### International Lesbian and Gay Association (ILGA)
www.ilga.org
Tel +32 2 5022471
Worldwide federation of several hundred national and local groups seeking equal rights for lesbians, gay men, bisexual and trans people.

### International Foundation for Gender Education (IFGE)
www.ifge.org
Advocates freedom for gender expression and promotes understanding and acceptance of all genders and orientations.

### International Gay and Lesbian Youth Organization (IGLYO)
www.iglyo.com
For gay, lesbian, transgender and queer youth and students worldwide.

### Amnesty International
www.ai-lgbt.org
Campaigns against human-rights abuses and discrimination around the world. Takes up individual cases.

### Human Rights Watch
www.hrw.org/lgbt
Documents and campaigns against human-rights abuses and discrimination around the world.

### OutRage
www.outrage.org.uk
UK-based but internationally focused direct action and campaign group. Contact point for Iraqi-LGBT.

### Al-Fatiha Foundation
www.al-fatiha.org
International organization for Muslims who are lesbian, gay, bisexual, transgendered or questioning.

### International Day Against Homophobia (IDAHO)
www.idahomophobia.org
For a universal decriminalization of homosexuality.

## REGIONAL groups and websites

### AFRICA AND MIDDLE EAST

### Behind the Mask
www.mask.opg.za
Website on gay and lesbian affairs in Africa including North Africa.

### Black Looks
www.blacklooks.org
African website tackling gender, sexuality, racism, HIV equality issues, with strong female perspective.

### Gay Middle East
www.gaymiddleeast.com
Country by country information with recent gay related news reports.

### Homan
www.homanla.org
Iranian gay, lesbian. bisexual and transgender organization and website, hosted in the US.

### Aswat
www.aswatgroup.org
Israel-based organization for Palestinian lesbians.

### EUROPE AND NORTH AMERICA

### Stonewall
www.stonewall.org
British group for lesbians, gay men and bisexuals.

### Press for Change
www.pfc.org.uk
UK-based group campaigning for respect and  equality for all transgender people.

### Egale (Equality for Gays and Lesbians)
www.egale.can
Canadian LGBT rights organization.

### National Gay and Lesbian Task Force
www.ngltf.org
US national campaign organization.

## Lesbian and Gay Immigration Rights Task Force
www.lgirtf.org
US-based immigration support.

## Genderpac
www.gpac.org
US national organization for gender freedom and transgender advocacy.

## The Intersex Society of North America (ISNA)
www.isna.org
Devoted to systemic change to end shame, secrecy, and unwanted genital surgeries for people with intersex conditions.

## Gay and Lesbian Arabic Society
www.glas.org
US-based organization aims to promote positive images of gays and lesbians in Arab communities worldwide and combats negative portrayal of Arabs within gay and lesbian communities.

### ASIA-PACIFIC

## South Asian Women's Organizations
www.sawnet.org/khush/
Excellent information and links for LGBT people living in South Asia and the diaspora.

## Naz Foundation
www.nazindia.org
HIV awareness and LGBT rights group spearheading bid to make homosexuality legal in India.

## Trikone
www.trikone.org
For LGBT of South Asian descent.

## Gay and Lesbian Rights Lobby
www.glrl.org.au
Australian campaign group.

### LATIN AMERICA AND THE CARIBBEAN

## Jamaica Forum of Lesbians, All Sexuals and Gays
www.jflag.org
Courageous LGBT activists campaigning for equality in a violent and hostile climate.

## MISCELLEANEOUS

## Safra Project
www.safraproject.org
Project working on issues relating to lesbian, bisexual and/or transgender women who identify as Muslim religiously and/or culturally.

## Lesbian and Gay Christian Movement
www.lgcm.org
UK-based campaign group.

## Queer Jihad
www.well.come/user/queerjhd
Website that condemns all forms of terrorism 'including prejudice and discrimination'.

## OTHER WEBSITES FOR INTERNATIONAL NEWS:
http://direland.typepad.com
www.gaycitynews.com
www.365.gay.com
www.planetout.com
www.utopia-asia.com
www.gay.com/news

# Appendix

F = female M = male LGBT: Lesbian, gay, bisexual and transgender
H = homosexuality T = transgender
G/r = gender reassignment ('sex change')

*Afghanistan* H: Illegal. F/M. Imprisonable for up to 15 years.
T: No data or legal situation unclear.

*Albania* H: Legal. Age of consent equal. LGBT citizens have been granted asylum by other countries.
T: G/r is illegal.

*Algeria* H: Illegal. F/M. Imprisonable for up to 3 years. LGBT citizens have been granted asylum by other countries. T: No data or legal situation unclear.

*Andorra* H: Legal. T: G/r is illegal.

*Angola* H: Illegal. F/M. T: No data or legal situation unclear.

*Antigua and Barbuda* H: Legal. T: No data or legal situation unclear.

*Argentina* H: Legal. Civil unions recognized in some regions. Anti-discrimination laws apply. Social intolerance can be extreme and LGBT citizens have been granted asylum by other countries. T: G/r legal or openly performed without prosecution.

*Armenia* H: Legal. Some residence rights for bi-national gay couples. LGBT citizens have been granted asylum by other countries, but now some support for LGBT refugees from elsewhere. T: No data or legal situation unclear.

*Aruba* H: Legal. Protection for sexual orientation under Dutch law but challenged by Arubian authorities. T: No data or legal situation unclear.

*Australia* H: Legal. Age of consent higher for gay men in some states. Anti-discrimination laws apply. Domestic partnership recognition in some states but federal ban on same-sex marriage. Same-sex adoption and donor insemination services available in some states. Prepared to grant asylum to LGBT refugees.
T: G/r legal in some states. Specific protection from discrimination exists for transgendered people.

*Austria* H: Legal. Anti-discrimination laws apply. Prepared to grant asylum to LGBT refugees. T: G/r legal or openly performed without prosecution. All personal documents may be reissued following change.

*Azerbaijan* H: Legal. Age of consent equal.
T: No data or legal situation unclear.

*Bahamas* H: Legal. Age of consent higher for lesbians and gay men. T: No data or legal situation unclear.

*Bahrain* H: Illegal. F/M. Imprisonable for up to 10 years; deportation for 20 years.
T: G/r illegal.

*Bangladesh* H: Illegal. F/M. Imprisonable for life. LGBT citizens have been granted asylum by other countries. T: No data or legal situation unclear.

*Barbados* H: Illegal. F/M. Imprisonable but rarely enforced against private behavior. Laws currently under review. T: No data or legal situation unclear.

*Belarus* H: Legal. Equal age of consent. But severe discrimination persists. T: G/r legal or openly performed without prosecution. No data on reissue of documents.

*Belgium* H: Legal. Age of consent equal. Same-sex couples can marry and adopt. Anti-discrimination laws apply. Prepared to grant asylum to LGBT refugees. T: G/r legal or openly performed without prosecution. All personal documents may be reissued following change.

*Belize* H: Illegal. F/M. Imprisonable for 10 years. T: No data or legal situation unclear.

*Benin* H: Illegal. F/M. T: No data or legal situation unclear.

*Bermuda* H: Legal. Higher age of consent.
T: No data or legal situation unclear.

*Bhutan* H: Illegal. F/M. Imprisonable for life. T: No data or legal situation unclear.

*Bolivia* H: Legal. No anti-discrimination laws. T: No data or legal situation unclear

*Bosnia & Herzegovina* H: Legal. Equal age of consent. Anti-discrimination laws apply. No legal recognition of same-sex partnerships. T: No data or legal situation unclear.

*Botswana* H: Illegal. M (F not mentioned in law). Imprisonable for 5 years. T: No data or legal situation unclear.

*Brazil* H: Legal. Equal age of consent. Anti discrimination and anti-vilification laws exist in several states; civil unions recognized in some. But high levels of homophobic violence; LGBT citizens have been granted asylum by other countries
T: G/r legal or openly performed without prosecution.

*Brunei* H: Illegal. F/M. Imprisonable for 10 years.T: No data or legal situation unclear.

*Bulgaria* H: Legal. Age of consent equal. Anti-discrimination laws apply. T: G/r legal or openly performed without prosecution.

*Burkina Faso* H: Legal. Age of consent equal. T: No data or legal situation unclear.

*Burma* H: Illegal. M (F not mentioned in law). Imprisonable for life. T: No data or legal situation unclear. Traditionally transgendered people have accepted place in society.

**Burundi H**: Illegal. M (F not known). Punishable as an 'immoral act'. **T**: No data or legal situation unclear.

**Cambodia H**: Legal. Age of consent equal. Former King Sihanouk has called for legalization of gay marriage. **T**: No data or legal situation unclear.

**Cameroon H**: Illegal. F/M. Imprisonable for 5 years. **T**: No data or legal situation unclear.

**Canada H**: Legal. Age of consent higher for anal sex (18). Legal recognition of same-sex partnerships, marriage and adoption rights. Constitutional laws against discrimination apply. Prepared to grant asylum to LGBT refugees. **T**: G/r legal in some states and provinces.

**Cape Verde H**: Illegal. F/M. 'Repeat offenders' may be imprisoned. **T**: No data or legal situation unclear.

**Cayman Islands H**: Legal. British laws apply. **T**: No data or legal situation unclear.

**Central African Republic H**: Legal. Age of consent equal. **T**: No data or legal situation unclear.

**Chad H**: Legal. Age of consent higher (18). **T**: No data or legal situation unclear.

**Chile H**: Legal. Age of consent higher (18). No anti-discrimination laws. LGBT citizens have been granted asylum by other countries. **T**: No data or legal situation unclear.

**China H**: Not illegal but considered 'unacceptable'. Legal in Hong Kong with equal age of consent. LGBT citizens from mainland China have been granted asylum by other countries. **T**: G/r legal or openly performed without prosecution.

**Colombia H**: Legal. Age of consent equal. Social intolerance can be extreme and LGBT citizens have been granted asylum by other countries. **T**: First country to restrict genital mutilation of intersex children without their, or before age of, consent.

**Cormoros H**: Legal. **T**: No data or legal situation unclear.

**Congo H**: Legal. Age of consent equal. **T**: No data or legal situation unclear.

**Congo Dem Rep H**: Illegal. F/M. Imprisonable for 5 years under 'crimes against the family' law. **T**: No data or legal situation unclear.

**Cook Islands H**: Illegal. M (F not mentioned in law). Imprisonable for 7 years. **T**: No data or legal situation unclear.

**Costa Rica H**: Legal, though 'scandalous' homosexuality illegal. Age of consent equal. Laws against discrimination apply but same-sex marriage is banned. **T**: No data or legal situation unclear.

**Croatia H**: Legal. Age of consent higher for lesbians and gay men (18). Registered

partnerships. LGBT citizens have been granted asylum by other countries. **T**: No data or legal situation unclear.

**Cuba H**: Legal but LGBT associations are banned. No laws against discrimination. LGBT citizens have been granted asylum by other countries. **T**: No data or legal situation unclear.

**Cyprus H**: Legal. Age of consent equal. **T**: No data or legal situation unclear.

**Czech Republic H**: Legal. Age of consent equal. Registered partnerships. Some anti-discrimination protection. **T**: G/r legal or openly performed without prosecution. Some personal documents may be reissued.

**Denmark H**: Legal. Age of consent equal. Legal recognition of same sex partnerships (also applies in Greenland) Legal recognition of non-biological parents. Anti-dicrimination laws apply. Prepared to grant asylum to LGBT refugees. **T**: G/r legal or openly performed without prosecution. All personal documents may be reissued following change.

**Djibouti H**: Illegal. F/M. **T**: No data or legal situation unclear.

**Dominican Republic H**: Legal. Age of consent equal. No laws against discrimination. **T**: No data or legal situation unclear. Cultural acceptance of transgendered guevedoche or 'pseudo-hermaphrodites'.

**Ecuador H**: Legal. Anti-discrimination written into the Constitution. Custody rights for lesbians. **T**: No data or legal situation unclear.

**Egypt H**: Technically legal but effectively illegal. A variety of laws are applied. **T**: G/r legal or openly performed without prosecution. Civil Law provisions exist for reissue of personal documents to reflect change.

**El Salvador H**: Legal. No laws against discrimination. LGBT citizens have been granted asylum by other countries. **T**: No data or legal situation unclear.

**Equatorial Guinea H**: Illegal. F/M. Imprisonable for 3 years. **T**: No data or legal situation unclear.

**Eritrea H**: Legal. M (F situation unclear). Age of consent 18. **T**: No data or legal situation unclear.

**Estonia H**: Legal. Age of consent equal. **T**: G/r legal or openly performed without prosecution. Documents cannot be reissued.

**Ethiopia H**: Illegal. F/M. Imprisonable for 3 years. **T**: No data or legal situation unclear.

**Fiji H**: Illegal. M (F not mentioned in law). Imprisonable for 14 years. Law has been ruled unconstitutional as Constitution protects against sexual orientation discrimination. **T**: No data or legal situation unclear.

**Finland H**: Legal. Age of consent equal. Registered partnerships. Anti-discrimination laws apply. Legal recognition of non-biological parents; access to state donor insemination services. Prepared to grant asylum to LGBT refugees. **T**: G/r legal or openly performed without prosecution. All personal documents may be reissued following change.

**France H**: Legal. Age of consent equal. Civil unions available to all regardless of sexual orientation. Anti-discrimination laws apply. Prepared to grant asylum to LGBT refugees. **T**: G/r legal or openly performed without prosecution. Some personal documents may be reissued after change.

**French Guyana H**: Legal. French laws apply. **T**: No data or legal situation unclear.

**Gabon H**: Legal. Age of consent higher for lesbians and gay men. **T**: No data or legal situation unclear.

**Gambia H**: Illegal. M (F situation unclear). Imprisonable for 14 years. **T**: No data or legal situation unclear.

**Georgia H**: Legal. Age of consent equal. Some anti-discrimination protection. **T**: G/r legal or openly performed without prosecution.

**Germany H**: Legal. Age of consent equal. Registered partnerships and adoption rights. Regional anti-discrimination laws apply. Prepared to grant asylum to LGBT refugees. **T**: G/r legal or openly performed without prosecution. All personal documents may be reissued after change.

**Ghana H**: Illegal. M. Punishable under 'unnatural carnal knowledge' laws. LGBT citizens have been granted asylum by other countries. **T**:G/r is illegal.

**Greece H**: Legal. Anti-discrimination in employment law applies. Access to state donor insemination services. Prepared to grant asylum to LGBT refugees. **T**: G/r legal or openly performed without prosecution. All personal documents may be reissued after change.

**Grenada H**: Illegal. M (F not mentioned in law). Imprisonable for 10 years. **T**: No data or legal situation unclear.

**Guam H**: Legal. No laws against discrimination. **T**: No data or legal situation unclear.

**Guatemala H**: Legal. Anti-discrimination laws apply. **T**: No data or legal situation unclear.

**Guinea H**: Illegal. F/M. Imprisonable for 3 years. **T**: No data or legal situation unclear.

**Guinea-Bissau H**: Legal. **T**: No data or legal situation unclear.

**Guyana H**: Illegal. M (F situation unclear).

Imprisonable for life. **T**: No data or legal situation unclear.

**Haiti H**: Legal. No laws against discrimination. **T**: No data or legal situation unclear.

**Honduras H**: Legal. Same-sex marriage and adoption by same-sex couples banned. LGBT citizens have been granted asylum by other countries. **T**: No data or legal situation unclear.

**Hungary H**: Legal. Legal recognition of same-sex partnerships. Anti-discrimination laws apply. **T**: G/r legal or openly performed without prosecution. Legal situation unclear on document issue.

**Iceland H**: Legal. Age of consent equal. Some legal protection for sexual orientation. Legal recognition of same-sex partnerships. Parenting: Legal recognition of non-biological parents. **T**: G/r legal or openly performed without prosecution. Legal situation unclear on document issue.

**India H**: Illegal. M (but law has been used against women and transsexuals too). Imprisonable for life, but provisions rarely applied. Judicial review of the law being sought. **T**: *Hijras* (eunuchs) can have ID cards changed to reflect female status.

**Indonesia H**: Legal. The Justice Ministry recently attempted to criminalize homosexuality. **T**: G/r legal or openly performed without prosecution. Transgender people have an accepted place in society.

**Iran H**: Illegal. F/M. Death penalty applies. In July 2005 two gay teenagers executed. Some 4,000 LGBT people are reported to have been executed since 1979. **T**: G/r is legal and government support available.

**Iraq H**: Situation unclear. Current Government has issued a decree allowing Sharia laws (death penalty for homosexuals) to be enforced. LGBT Iraqis are now targeted for persecution and execution. **T**: No data or legal situation unclear.

**Ireland H**: Legal. Age of consent equal. Anti-discrimination laws apply. Prepared to grant asylum to LGBT refugees. **T**: G/r legal or openly performed without prosecution. It is illegal to change birth certificate or marry after gender reassignment.

**Israel H**: Legal. Age of consent equal. Some legal protection for sexual orientation, including within the armed forces. **T**: G/r legal or openly performed without prosecution.

**Italy H**: Legal. Age of consent equal. Civil unions in some regions. **T**: G/r legal or openly performed without prosecution. Some personal documents may be reissued after change.

**Ivory Coast H**: Legal. Age of consent

higher. **T:** No data or legal situation unclear.

**Jamaica H:** Illegal. M (F not mentioned in law). Imprisonable for 10 years (can be accompanied by hard labor). High level of social intolerance and violence towards LGBT people. **T:** No data or legal situation unclear.

**Japan H:** Legal. **T:** G/r legal or openly performed without prosecution. All personal documents may be reissued after change.

**Jordan H:** Legal. But LGBT citizens at risk of vigilante 'honor' killing and have been granted asylum by other countries. **T:** No data or legal situation unclear.

**Kazakhstan H:** Legal. No anti-discrimination laws. **T:** No data or legal situation unclear.

**Kenya H:** Illegal. M (F not mentioned in law). Imprisonable for 14 years. **T:** No data or legal situation unclear. Traditionally transgendered people had an accepted place in society.

**Kiribati H:** Illegal. M (F not mentioned in law). Imprisonable for 14 years. **T:** No data or legal situation unclear.

**Korea, N H:** Legal. **T:** No data or legal situation unclear.

**Korea, S H:** Legal. Anti-discrimination law exists but Government continues to discriminate. **T:** No data or legal situation unclear.

**Kosovar Autonomus Region H:** Illegal. M. **T:** No data or legal situation unclear.

**Kuwait H:** Illegal. F/M. Imprisonable for 7 years. Laws denying freedom of expression and/or association also apply. **T:** No data or legal situation unclear.

**Kyrgyzstan H:** Legal. No anti-discrimination laws. **T:** No data or legal situation unclear.

**Laos H:** Unclear as to whether acts in private between consenting adults are legal or not. **T:** No data or legal situation unclear.

**Latvia H:** Legal. Same-sex marriages banned. No anti-discrimination laws. Prepared to grant asylum to LGBT refugees **T:** G/r legal or openly performed without prosecution. Some personal documents may be reissued after change.

**Lebanon H:** Illegal. F/M. Imprisonable for 1 year. Laws denying freedom of expression and association apply. LGBT citizens have been granted asylum by other countries **T:** No data or the situation unclear.

**Lesotho H:** Legal. Homosexuality not mentioned in law. **T:** No data or legal situation unclear.

**Liberia H:** Illegal. F/M. **T:** No data or legal situation unclear.

**Libya H:** Illegal. F/M. Imprisonable for 5 years. **T:** No data or legal situation unclear.

**Liechtenstein H:** Legal. Age of consent

equal. Laws against discrimination apply. **T:** No data or legal situation unclear.

**Lithuania H:** Legal. Age of consent equal. Some legal protection against discrimination. **T:** Gender reassignment illegal.

**Luxembourg H:** Legal. Age of consent equal. Registered same-sex partnerships. Laws against discrimination apply. **T:** G/r legal or openly performed without prosecution. Some personal documents may be reissued after change.

**Macedonia (TFYR) H:** Legal. No laws against discrimination. Gays barred from entering legal profession. **T:** G/r is illegal.

**Madagascar H:** Legal. **T:** No data or legal situation unclear. Transgendered people have an accepted place in society.

**Malawi H:** Illegal. F/M. **T:** No data or legal situation unclear.

**Malaysia H:** Illegal. M (situation unclear for F). Imprisonable for 20 years. LGBT citizens have been granted asylum by other countries. **T:** Gender reassignment is recognized but right to marry denied.

**Maldives H:** Illegal. M (F not mentioned in law). Imprisonable for life. Trangender rights: No data or legal situation unclear.

**Mali H:** No laws against, but LGBT may be prosecuted under 'Public Morals' law. **T:** No data or legal situation unclear.

**Malta H:** Legal. Age of consent equal. **T:** No data or legal situation unclear.

**Marshall Islands H:** Illegal. M (F not mentioned in law). Imprisonable for 10 years. **T:** No data or legal situation unclear.

**Martinique H:** Legal. French laws apply. **T:** No data or legal situation unclear.

**Mauritania H:** Illegal. F/M. Death penalty applies. LGBT citizens have been granted asylum by other countries. **T:** No data or legal situation unclear.

**Mauritius H:** Illegal. F/M. Imprisonable for 3 years. **T:** No data or legal situation unclear.

**Mexico H:** Legal. Laws against discrimination apply. Social intolerance can be extreme and LGBT citizens have been granted asylum by other countries. **T:** No data or legal situation unclear.

**Micronesia, fed States of H:** Not mentioned in law. **T:** No data or legal situation unclear.

**Moldova, Rep of H:** Legal. **T:** G/r legal or openly performed without prosecution. All personal documents may be reissued following change.

**Monaco H:** Legal. Age of consent equal. **T:** G/r legal or openly performed without prosecution. All personal documents may be reissued following change.

**Mongolia H:** Not mentioned in law

but penal code prohibiting 'immoral gratification of sexual desires' is used against gay people. **T**: No data or legal situation unclear.

**Morocco H**: Illegal. F/M. Imprisonable for 3 years. LGBT citizens have been granted asylum by other countries. **T**: Legal situation unclear.

**Mozambique H**: Illegal. F/M. Imprisonable for 3 years with hard labor. **T**: No data or legal situation unclear.

**Namibia H**: Illegal. M (situation unclear for F). Legal precedent gave immigration rights to same-sex lesbian partnership. Some anti-discrimination provision applies, in spite of illegality. **T**: Gender reassignment recognized. Documents can be changed on social acceptance.

**Naura H**: Legal situation unclear. **T**: No data or legal situation unclear.

**Nepal H**: Illegal. F/M. Imprisonable for life. Law being challenged in Supreme Court. **T**: No data or legal situation unclear.

**Netherlands H**: Legal. Age of consent equal. Same-sex civil unions and marriages performed. Anti-discrimination laws apply. Legal recognition of non-biological parents and same-sex adoption rights. Access to state donor insemination services. Prepared to grant asylum to LGBT refugees. **T**: G/r legal or openly performed without prosecution. Some personal documents may be reissued after change.

**Netherland Antilles H**: Legal. Dutch law applies but while same-sex civil unions and marriages are recognized they cannot be performed. **T**: No data or legal situation unclear.

**New Zealand H**: Legal. Age of consent equal. Legal protection for sexual orientation under the Human Rights Act. Same-sex civil unions recognized. Prepared to grant asylum to LGBT refugees. **T**: G/r legal or openly performed without prosecution. All official documents may be reissued to reflect change.

**Nicaragua H**: Illegal. F/M. Imprisonable for 3 years. Law is being challenged in the High Court. LGBT citizens have been granted asylum by other countries. **T**: No data or legal situation unclear.

**Niger H**: Legal. Age of consent 21. Same-sex marriages are allowed. **T**: No data or legal situation unclear.

**Nigeria H**: Illegal. M (F not mentioned in law). Imprisonable for 14 years. In Northern provinces death penalty under Sharia law applies. A new law forbids same-sex marriage and prohibits gays from assembling and petitioning the government. It also allows prosecution of newspapers that publish information about same-sex

relationships and religious groups that allow same-sex unions. Those who violate the law can be sentenced to 5 years in prison. **T**: No data or legal situation unclear.

**Niue H**: Illegal. M (F not mentioned in law). Imprisonable for 10 years. **T**: No data or legal situation unclear.

**Norway H**: Legal. Age of consent equal. Legal recognition of same-sex partnerships. Legal recognition of non-biological parents. Prepared to grant asylum to LGBT refugees. **T**: G/r legal or openly performed without prosecution. Some personal documents may be reissued to reflect change.

**Oman H**: Illegal. (F/M). Imprisonable for 3 years. **T**: No data or legal situation unclear. Transgendered people have an accepted place.

**Pakistan H**: Illegal. F/M. Death penalty applies under Sharia law. LGBT citizens have been granted asylum by other countries. **T**: Some official recognition of gender reassignment and right to marry subsequently.

**Palestinian Authority H**: Not illegal but LGBT people targeted. Many leave for Israel. **T**: No data or legal situation unclear.

**Panama H**: Legal. **T**: G/r ('sex change') legal or openly performed without prosecution. Some personal documents may be reissued to reflect change.

**Papua New Guinea H**: Illegal. M (F not mentioned in law). Imprisonable for 14 years. **T**: No data or legal situation unclear.

**Paraguay H**: Legal. Age of consent equal. No anti-discrimination laws. **T**: No data or legal situation unclear.

**Peru H**: Legal. Some anti-discrimination protection applies. LGBT citizens have been granted asylum by other countries. **T**: No data or legal situation unclear.

**Philippines H**: Legal. Age of consent equal. Same-sex marriage banned. **T**: G/r legal or openly performed without prosecution.

**Poland H**: Legal. Age of consent equal. High level of social intolerance. LGBT citizens have been granted asylum by other countries. **T**: G/r legal or openly performed without prosecution. Some personal documents may be reissued to reflect change.

**Portugal H**: Legal. Age of consent equal. Same-sex civil unions allowed but not same-sex adoption. **T**: G/r legal or openly performed without prosecution. Personal documents may be reissued to reflect change.

**Qatar H**: Illegal. F/M. Imprisonable for up to 5 years. **T**: No data or legal situation unclear.

**Romania H**: Legal. Some anti-discrimination protection. **T**: G/r legal or openly performed without prosecution. Some personal documents may be reissued to reflect change.

**Russian Federation H:** Legal in all states except Chechyna (where the death penalty applies under Sharia law). Age of consent equal. Three attempts to recriminalize homosexuality in Russia between 2002 and 2004 failed. LGBT citizens have been granted asylum in other countries. **T:** G/r legal or openly performed without prosecution. All personal documents may be reissued to reflect change. Traditionally, transgender people had an accepted place in Siberian society.

**Rwanda H:** Legal. Age of consent higher. **T:** No data or legal situation unclear.

**Saint Kitts and Nevis H:** Illegal. M (F not mentioned in law). Imprisonable for 10 years. **T:** No data or legal situation unclear.

**Saint Lucia H:** Illegal. M. (F not mentioned in law). Imprisonable for 10 years. **T:** No data or legal situation unclear.

**Saint Vincent/Grenadines H:** Illegal. F/M. Imprisonable for 10 years. **T:** No data or legal situation unclear.

**Sao Tome and Principe H:** Illegal. F/M. **T:** No data or legal situation unclear.

**Saudi Arabia H:** Illegal. F/M. Death penalty, imprisonment and flogging under Sharia law. Executions have taken place during past 10 years. **T:** No data or legal situation unclear.

**Senegal H:** Illegal. F/M. **T:** No data or legal situation unclear.

**Serbia (TFYR) H:** Legal. Age of consent higher for male homosexual anal sex (18). **T:** No data or legal situation unclear.

**Seychelles H:** Illegal. M (F not mentioned in law). **T:** No data or legal situation unclear.

**Sierra Leone H:** Illegal. M (situation unclear for F). **T:** No data or legal situation unclear.

**Singapore H:** Illegal. M (F not mentioned in law). Imprisonable for life but law rarely enforced. LGBT citizens have been granted asylum by other countries. **T:** G/r legal or openly performed without prosecution.

**Slovakia H:** Legal. Same-sex registered partnerships. Anti-discrimination laws apply. **T:** G/r legal or openly performed without prosecution. Some personal documents may be reissued to reflect change.

**Slovenia H:** Legal. Same-sex registered partnerships. Anti-discrimination laws apply. **T:** No data or legal situation unclear.

**Solomon Islands H:** Legal. F/M. Imprisonable for up to 14 years. **T:** No data or legal situation unclear.

**Somalia H:** Illegal. F/M. Death penalty in some areas ruled by sharia law and applies to both women and men. Imprisonable for up to 3 years. **T:** No data or legal situation unclear.

**South Africa H:** Legal. First country in the world to include equality and sexual orientation protection in its Constitution. Age of consent higher (19). Same-sex marriage and adoption of children allowed. Prepared to grant asylum to LGBT refugees. **T:** G/r legal or openly performed without prosecution. Personal documents may be reissued to reflect change.

**Spain H:** Legal. Age of consent equal. Same-sex marriage and adoption of children allowed. Anti-discrimination laws apply. Access to state donor insemination services. **T:** G/r legal or openly performed without prosecution. All personal documents may be reissued to reflect change.

**Sri Lanka H:** Illegal. M (F not mentioned in law). Imprisonable for 10 years. **T:** No data or legal situation unclear.

**Sudan H:** Illegal. F/M. Death penalty applies under sharia law or 5 years' imprisonment. **T:** No data or legal situation unclear.

**Suriname H:** Legal but severe discrimination in criminal law. Age of consent higher (18). **T:** No data or legal situation unclear.

**Swaziland H:** Illegal. F/M. Imprisonment and/or fine. **T:** No data or legal situation unclear.

**Sweden H:** Legal. Age of consent equal. Anti-discrimination laws apply. Legal recognition of same-sex partnerships and adoption of children allowed. Access to state donor insemination services. Prepared to grant asylum to LGBT refugees. **T:** G/r legal or openly performed without prosecution. All personal documents may be reissued to reflect change.

**Switzerland H:** Legal. Age of consent equal. Registered same-sex partnerships. Anti-discrimination on the basis of 'lifestyle' clause in the Constitution. But no access to state donor insemination for lesbians. **T:** G/r legal or openly performed without prosecution. All personal documents may be reissued to reflect change.

**Syria H:** Illegal. F/M. Imprisonable for up to 3 years. LGBT citizens have been granted asylum by other countries. **T:** No data or legal situation unclear.

**Taiwan H:** Legal. Age of consent equal. Pending law allows for same-sex marriage. **T:** G/r legal or openly performed without prosecution.

**Tajikistan H:** Illegal. M (F not mentioned in law). **T:** No data or legal situation unclear.

**Tanzania H:** Illegal. F/M. Imprisonable

for life. New laws have crimininalized lesbianism and made same-sex marriage illegal and imprisonable for 7 years. LGBT citizens have applied for asylum in other countries. **T**: No data or legal situation unclear.

*Thailand* **H**: Legal. Age of consent equal. **T**: G/r legal or openly performed without prosecution.

*Timor Leste (East Timor)* **H**: Legal. **T**: No data or legal situation unclear.

*Togo* **H**: Illegal. F/M. Imprisonable for up to 3 years. **T**: No data or legal situation unclear.

*Tokelau* **H**: Illegal. M (F not mentioned in law). Imprisonable for 10 years. **T**: No data or legal situation unclear.

*Tonga* **H**: Illegal. M (F not mentioned in law). Imprisonable for up to 10 years. **T**: No data or legal situation unclear.

*Trinidad and Tobago* **H**: Illegal. F/M. Imprisonable for 10 years. **T**: No data or legal situation unclear.

*Tunisia* **H**: Illegal. F/M. Imprisonable for up to 3 years. LGBT citizens have been granted asylum by other countries. **T**: Rights only for born-hermaphrodites.

*Turkey* **H**: Legal. Age of consent equal. Lesbians and gay men are banned from the armed forces. LGBT citizens have been granted asylum by other countries. **T**: G/r legal or openly performed without prosecution. All personal documents may be reissued to reflect change.

*Turkmenistan* **H**: Illegal. M (F not mentioned in law). Imprisonable for 3 years. **T**: No data or legal situation unclear.

*Turks and Caicos* **H**: Legal. **T**: No data or legal situation unclear.

*Tuvalu* **H**: Illegal. M (F not mentioned in law). Imprisonable for 14 years. **T**: No data or legal situation unclear.

*Uganda* **H**: Illegal. M (F not mentioned in law, but has been used against women). Imprisonable for life. In 2005 same-sex marriage was criminalized. LGBT citizens have been granted asylum in other countries. **T**: No data or legal situation unclear.

*Ukraine* **H**: Legal. Age of consent equal. No anti-discrimination laws. **T**: G/r legal or openly performed without prosecution. All personal documents may be reissued to reflect change.

*United Arab Emirates* **H**: Illegal. M (situation for F unclear). Death sentence applies. In 2006 11 men imprisoned for 5 years for attending a 'gay wedding'. **T**: No data or legal situation unclear.

*United Kingdom* **H**: Legal. Age of consent equal. Anti-discrimination laws apply. Same-sex civil unions recognized in 2005. Same-sex couples allowed to adopt in some areas.

Prepared to grant asylum to LGBT refugees. **T**: G/r legal or openly performed without prosecution. All personal documents may be reissued to reflect change.

*United States* **H**: Legal. In 2003 a US Supreme Court ruling overturned anti-sodomy laws which applied in 20 states. Progressive anti-discrimination laws and legal recognition of same-sex partnerships apply in some states and municipalities. Same-sex couples can adopt in some states. Prepared to grant asylum to LGBT refugees. **T**: G/r legal or openly performed without prosecution in some states. Personal documents may be reisssued to reflect change in most states. Traditional Native American acceptance of transgender.

*Uruguay* **H**: Legal. Anti-discrimination laws apply. **T**: No data or legal situation unclear.

*Uzbekistan* **H**: Illegal. M (F not mentioned in law). Imprisonable for three years. LGBT citizens have been granted asylum by other countries. **T**: No data or legal situation unclear.

*Vanuatu* **H**: Legal. **T**: No data or legal situation unclear.

*Vatican/Holy See* **H**: Technically legal but de facto forbidden. **T**: Condemned as 'repugnant'.

*Venezuela* **H**: Legal. Anti-discrimination laws apply. Social intolerance can be extreme and LGBT citizens have been granted asylum by other countries **T**: No data or legal situation unclear.

*Vietnam* **H**: Legal. Age of consent equal. Same-sex marriage banned since 1998. **T**: No data or legal situation unclear.

*Western Samoa* **H**: Illegal. F/M. Imprisonable for 7 years. **T**: No data or legal situation unclear. Some traditional acceptance of transgender people.

*Yemen* **H**: Illegal. F/M. Death penalty applies. **T**: No data or legal situation unclear.

*Zambia* **H**: Illegal. M (F not mentioned in law). Imprisonable for 14 years. **T**: No data or legal situation unclear.

*Zimbabwe* **H**: Illegal. M. (F not mentioned in law). Pro-LGBT clergy risk imprisonment. LGBT citizens have been granted asylum in other countries. **T**: No data or legal situation unclear.

**Sources**: International Gay and Lesbian Human Rights Commission (**IGLHRC**) 2006 Web: www. iglhrc.org; International Lesbian and Gay Association *World Survey* (**ILGA**) 2006 Web: www.ilga.org; *LGBT world legal wrap up survey*, compiled by Daniel Ottosson, ILGA, November 2006, www.ilga.org/ statehomophobia/World_legal_wrap_up_

survey_November2006.pdf Sodomy Laws www.sodomylaws.org Behind the Mask 2006 web: www.mask.org.za Amnesty International AI-LGBT website www. ai-lgbt.org/status_worldwide.htm *Sex, Love and Homophobia* by Vanessa Baird, Amnesty International, 2004. Press for Change Web: www.pfc.org.uk *Integrating Transexual and Transgendered People: A Comparative Study of European, Commonwealth and International Law*, last modified 2004 available on http://www.pfc.org.uk/liga/liba-4a6.htm
**Notes**:

1 Legality and social or cultural acceptance are not necessarily related.
2 Where there are no specific laws against homosexuality, other laws may used against LGBT people.
3 Laws against male homosexuality may also be used against lesbians in some countries.
4 In the countries of the European Union cases of discrimination against sexual minorities can be challenged by referring to the Human Rights Act of 2000 providing another right has also been breached.

Laws concerning the status of LGBT people are not always clear and subject to change. Any updates, corrections or amendments will be gratefully received by Vanessa Baird on vanessab@newint.org

# Bibliography

*Born Gay? The Psychobiology of Sex Orientation*, Glenn Wilson and Quzi Rahman, Peter Owen, 2004

*Born to be Gay: A history of homosexuality* William G Naphy, NPI Media Group, 2006

Cassell's *Encyclopedia of Queer Myth, Symbol and Spirit*, Randy P Conner, David Hatfield Sparks, Mariya Sparks eds, 1997

*Crimes of Hate, Conspiracies of Silence*, Amnesty International, 2001

*Different Rainbows*, Peter Drucker ed, Gay Men's Press, 2000

*Facing the Mirror: Lesbian writing from India*, Ashwini Sukthankar, Penguin, 1999

*Female Desires: same sex relations and transgender practice across cultures*, Evelyn Blackwood and Saskia E Wieringa eds, Columbia University Press, 1999

*Gay Life and Culture: a World History*, Robert Aldrich ed, Thames and Hudson, 2006

*Global Sex*, Dennis Altman, University of Chicago Press, 2001

*Hidden from History*, Martin Bauml Duberman, Martha Vicinus, George Chauncey eds, Penguin, 1989

*Homophobia*, Byrne Fone, Metropolitan Books, 2000

*Homosexualities*, Stephen O Murray, University of Chicago Press, 2000

*Love in a Different Climate: men who have sex with men in India*, Jeremy Seabrook, Verso, 1999

*Loving Women: Being Lesbian in Unprivileged India*, Maya Sharma, Yoda Press, 2006

*Queer Science: the Use and Abuse of Research into Homosexuality*, Simon Le Vay, MIT Press, 1996

*Reclaiming Genders: transsexual grammars at the fin de siècle*, Kate More and Stephen Whittle eds, Cassell, 1999

*Sex, Love and Homophobia*, Vanessa Baird, Amnesty International, 2004

*Sexuality: second edition*, Jeffrey Weeks, Routledge, 2003

*Social Perspectives in Lesbian and Gay Studies: a reader*, Peter M Nardi and Beth E Schneider eds, Routledge, 1998

*The Global Emergence of Gay and Lesbian Politics*, Barry D Adam et al eds, Temple University Press, 1999

*The History of Sexuality*, Michel Foucault, Penguin Books, 1976

*The Men of the Pink Triangle*, Heinz Heger, Gay Men's Press, 1972

*The Mismeasurement of Desire: the science, theory and ethics of sexual orientation*, Edward Stein, Oxford University Press, 1999

*The Myth of the Modern Homosexual*, Rictor Norton, Cassell, 1997

*The New Gay Teenager*, Ritch C Savin-Williams, Harvard University Press, 2006.

*The Penguin Atlas of Human Sexual Behavior*, Judith Mackay, Penguin, 2000

*Third Sex, Third Gender*, Gilbert Herdt ed, Zone Books 1993

*Trans Liberation*, Leslie Feinberg, Beacon Press, 1998

*Unspeakable Love: Gay and Lesbian Life in the Middle East*, Brian Whitaker, Saqi, 2006

# Index